STOP OVERTHINKING AND BOOST YOUR MOOD

STOP OVERTHINKING AND BOOST YOUR MOOD

A 21-DAY GUIDE TO COPING, CONFIDENCE, AND CALM

by Kathleen Evans, LMHC

Copyright © March 2025
First edition

Stop Overthinking and Boost Your Mood: A 21-day Guide to Coping, Confidence, and Calm is designed to provide accurate, reliable information on the subject matter covered.

Specific names, identifying characteristics, and details have been changed to protect the privacy of individuals. Any resemblance to actual persons, living or dead, is coincidental.

It is intended as a self-guided supplement for healthy emotional care, not a medical replacement. The author offers helpful suggestions based on her experience and does not provide medical advice or counseling. She does not mean for her advice to replace the practice of medicine, including, but not limited to, psychiatry, psychology, psychotherapy, the provision of health care, diagnosis or treatment, or the creation of a mentor-mentee or coaching relationship.

If you use any of the information within this guide, the author does not assume or accept any responsibility for your actions or their consequences. You are encouraged to use independent research and discuss what you've read with your doctor, psychiatrist, therapist, sponsor, or counselor, or confidants before making any major life changes based on the contents of this book.

No part of this publication may be reproduced, distributed, or transmitted in any form or by any means, including photocopying, recording, or other electronic or mechanical methods, without the publisher's prior written permission, except as permitted by U.S. copyright law.

Softcover ISBN: 979-8-218-87752-1

Cover Designer: Danielle Kane
Photograph provided by the author
Diagrams from Shutterstock

TABLE OF CONTENTS

Introduction 1

Chapter 1: Brain Neuroscience 101 11

Chapter 2: Mindful Awareness 27

Chapter 3: Authentic Confident Self 57

Chapter 4: Coping with the Emotional & Cognitive Storms........... 81

Chapter 5: Stop Overthinking: Thought Pausing Tools................ 151

Chapter 6: Finding and Maintaining Healthy Relationships......... 163

Chapter 7: Brain Mood Boosts! 177

The 21-Day Accountability Journal.. 197

End-of-Journal Reflection: Noticing Changes in Thoughts, Emotions, and Overall Well-Being... 224

References 232

Meet the Author 239

Introduction

I sat across from James in my small counseling office, noticing a slight tinge of fear under the compassion I felt for him. James was tattooed, muscular, and very angry. He was also successful, handsome, and smart, and was attending weekly therapy sessions with me to help manage his anger issues. However, no matter how much he wanted to change, his brain would short-circuit into old rageful patterns whenever he was triggered, in or out of counseling.

For forty years of his life, James had never been taught how to process and express anger in healthy ways, and he had developed intense reactivity patterns: First, he would experience a triggering event, then he would react with habitual, unhealthy responses. Noticing his deeply wired pattern, I saw the commonality in how we all habitually respond to stress, reacting to our own triggers with anxious, depressing or rageful reflexes. It was in that moment I wanted to hand James a book—one with specific, actionable steps he could take to express his anger instead of relying on the old habits which were not working.

None of the psychology books I had read in my training fit the bill. Instead, James and I wrote our own simplified plan to disrupt his anger patterns. We identified and agreed upon behaviors James could take right after he noticed his rage button flip on. With these coping skills in hand, and with mindfulness, confidence-building and practice, James would aim to retrain his brain to respond to stress with adaptive, healthy skills.

Our plan worked. James started pausing before reacting, started self-regulating in times of high stress, and grew calmer and closer with his wife and children.

THERE WAS A PATTERN

Over time, I saw a similar roadmap for change emerging with other clients just like James. As this pattern for success repeated itself over and over again in the therapeutic process, the chapters of this book started to emerge.

When I eventually left my private practice and moved to a college counseling center, I noticed another recurring pattern while working with students. I would often ask high-achieving young adults, "What coping strategies do you use to manage your stress and anxiety?" The response was almost always a shrug followed by, "I don't really have any."

These students, I realized, were a lot like James. It's not that they didn't want to manage their emotions—it's that many of them were never taught how. And the more I encountered this vital gap in my sessions, the more I realized how widespread the problem really is.

From a young age, we are all taught the importance of physical hygiene, while emotional hygiene is rarely emphasized. We learn to brush our teeth, wash our hair, eat healthy foods, and exercise our bodies, but when it comes to caring for our emotional well-being, many of us never receive similar guidance.

That's what this book seeks to change.

EMOTIONAL AND COGNITIVE HYGIENE

Emotional and cognitive hygiene can be defined as the daily practice of choosing to create positive emotions while soothing and resolving negative emotions in a healthy way.

Just as brushing your teeth helps prevent cavities, regular emotional care can prevent mental health crises from escalating.

We are all living in times of heightened mental health crises. Anxiety, depression, and loneliness are more widespread than ever before. In the U.S. alone, mental health care expenses surpass three trillion dollars annually, with most of that spending going toward managing existing issues rather than preventing new ones. Despite this staggering investment, countless individuals—particularly young people—still find themselves feeling lost and unsupported. Suicide has tragically become the second leading cause of death among youth.

Fortunately, modern psychology and neuroscience offer us tools to regulate our over-triggered nervous systems. The purpose of this workbook is to distill those tools into practical strategies you can use every day, pulled from my years of experience helping clients like James. Another purpose of this book? Access. Waitlists in college counseling centers and private practices can be months to years. Barriers ranging from cost, to stigma, to fear of judgment are innumerable. Following our roadmap to change will help you, hopefully just as a trusted therapist would, without the logistical hassles.

This book mirrors what a short-term therapy plan might look like. Each chapter builds upon the previous one, offering psychoeducation and practical tools that you can apply right away, with both immediate and long-term results.

Think of the process as training for your mind, just like you would train your muscles at the gym. The goal is simple: *to help grow gray matter in the "feel-good" parts of your brain while calming the regions responsible for stress.* By practicing the tools we will discuss, repetition and discipline will lead to astonishing mental strength over time. With consistent practice, you'll notice real changes in how you think and feel.

HERE'S WHAT YOU CAN EXPECT TO LEARN BY WORKING THROUGH THIS BOOK:

- How to strengthen your connection to the present moment.
- How to rediscover your Authentic Confident Self (ACS).
- Techniques to reduce and manage uncomfortable emotions.
- Ways to cultivate positive emotions and boost your mood naturally.
- Practical strategies to increase the brain's "feel-good" chemicals: dopamine, serotonin, oxytocin, and endorphins.
- How to save time, energy, and money by becoming your own short-term therapist.

YOU MIGHT BE WONDERING, "WHAT'S THE DIFFERENCE BETWEEN SHORT-TERM AND LONG-TERM THERAPY?"

The answer lies in their goals and duration.

Short-term therapy, sometimes called solution-focused therapy, usually lasts a few weeks to a few months. It's designed to provide quick relief by addressing immediate concerns with practical strategies.

Unlike **long-term therapy**, which often involves deep exploration of past experiences and unconscious patterns, short-term therapy focuses on the present—on developing skills to manage current stressors.

Both approaches have their merits. Long-term therapy is valuable for those who need deeper healing or want to unravel complex psychological issues. However, not everyone has the luxury of time and money to engage in long-term counseling. That's where short-term therapy comes in.

A Crash Course in Emotional Fitness

Short-term therapy is an intensive, focused approach to managing life's ups and downs.

It is designed to provide immediate relief and actionable solutions. Imagine you're walking through a forest and suddenly find yourself lost in a thick fog. Long-term therapy would help you figure out how you got there in the first place—perhaps tracing your path, understanding why you made certain turns, and helping you avoid similar situations in the future. Short-term therapy, on the other hand, hands you a flashlight. It may not solve every deep, underlying problem, but it gives you the tools to navigate your immediate surroundings and find your way out of the fog.

This book takes that flashlight approach. We won't sit for hours analyzing the past or unraveling deep fears. Instead, we will work through clear, focused exercises to help you manage what's in front of you—whether that's anxiety about a work deadline, worry about a relationship, or frustration over being ghosted. You'll learn how to recognize when your emotions are taking over, how to calm your nervous system, and how to respond from a place of clarity rather than reactivity.

If you're anything like James and countless students from my university practice (and in my experience, most of us are), you struggle with waves of anxiety, anger, sadness, or other complex emotions that stop you in your tracks. Fortunately, an immediate, actionable roadmap toward strengthening your emotional hygiene in real time could vastly improve how you navigate the world and its challenges.

Welcome. This book is for you.

LET'S BREAK IT DOWN

Each chapter is designed to guide you step-by-step toward greater emotional clarity, resilience, and balance. Here' a snapshot to help orient you on the path:

In Chapter 1, we'll begin by exploring the basics of neuroscience. You'll learn about key parts of the brain involved in emotional regulation—like the prefrontal cortex and the amygdala—and how they interact during moments of stress or calm. Understanding these processes will empower you to take control of your emotional responses, rather than feeling controlled by them.

Chapter 2 introduces mindfulness, a practice that helps you develop awareness of your thoughts and emotions without judgment. Think of mindfulness as the sky—ever-present, unchanging backdrop, able to hold whatever weather (emotions) may come your way. We will review practical, easy ways to practice mindfulness daily.

In Chapter 3, we'll focus on building your Authentic Confident Self. Confidence is like the sun—always shining, even when it's obscured by temporary clouds of doubt or fear. Through exercises and reflection, you'll learn how to reconnect with the core version of yourself that feels strong and capable.

Next, in Chapter 4, we'll dive into emotional regulation. You'll discover effective coping skills for dealing with common uncomfortable emotions, including sadness, worry, self-doubt, and anger. Each section will provide tools to help you soothe these emotional storms when they arise.

By Chapter 5, we'll move on to thought-pausing techniques—strategies designed to help you break free from overthinking and enjoy the present moment more fully. Whether it's racing thoughts about the future or rumination about the past, these tools will help you find calm amidst mental chatter.

In Chapter 6, you'll learn how to build and maintain healthy interpersonal relationships. As social creatures, our brains are impacted by those who we surround ourselves with. Some can be a resource, offering us empathy, kindness, or humor, while others can be a constant drain, triggering our own *fight, flight or freeze* responses due to their own toxicity of words and actions. Learning how our brain wiring can impact our high-stakes relationships can help with effective communication and healthier interpersonal connections.

In Chapter 7, you'll learn how to boost your brain's natural feel-good chemicals through simple daily

habits. From practicing gratitude to engaging in physical movement, these strategies are easy to implement and are highly effective.

THE GOAL OF THIS APPROACH IS SIMPLICITY.

There's no need for fancy equipment or complicated routines. All you need is yourself, a willingness to try, and a few minutes each day. The exercises in this book aren't demanding—they're small, manageable practices that fit into your daily life. Whether it's taking a mindful breath while brushing your teeth, repeating an affirmation during a morning walk, or pausing a racing thought before it spirals, these little moments add up. They create what neuroscientists call *micro-shifts*—tiny, incremental changes in your brain's wiring that, over time, lead to significant changes in moods and thought patterns.

This book is designed to be a self-paced journey. You can move through it at whatever speed feels right for you. You might choose to work through a chapter a week or take things slower, spending a couple of weeks on each section. The important thing is to stay consistent—because consistency is what leads to lasting change.

Your brain is adaptable. Your emotions aren't permanent. You don't have to stay stuck in old patterns.

> **What you focus on grows, and not just metaphorically—neurobiologically, as physical patterns in the brain.**

With practice, you can train yourself to respond to life's challenges with greater calm, clarity, and confidence.

This book is your invitation to start fresh, to build a new relationship with your thoughts and emotions, and to create a life that feels more peaceful, more authentic, and more *you*.

So, grab a pen, take a deep breath, and let's go!

Chapter 1: Brain Neuroscience 101

Understand How Your Brain Works

Imagine trying to fix a broken machine without knowing how its parts work. You could poke around, maybe tighten a few screws here and there. But without understanding how the pieces fit together, you'd have a tough time solving the problem. The same goes for your brain. To improve the way it reacts to stress or anxiety, you first need to understand the key players involved—the parts of your brain responsible for regulation and dysregulation. Understanding why our brains go into panic or shutdown mode from a technical standpoint can also be helpful in normalizing the experience and decreasing self-blame.

Once you've grasped these basics, you'll be better equipped to rewire those patterns and reclaim control over your thoughts and emotions.

In this chapter, we'll focus on three crucial components of your brain.

- The Prefrontal Cortex (PFC)
- The Amygdala, and Neurons
- The Neurotransmitters They Produce.

Understanding these parts and how they interact will give you a clearer picture of why you feel overwhelmed in stressful situations—and more importantly, how you can change that response.

THE PREFRONTAL CORTEX (PFC): YOUR BRAIN'S CEO

At the front of your brain lies the prefrontal cortex, often referred to as the brain's *executive center*. Think of it as the rational, level-headed CEO of your mind, responsible for critical functions like:

- **Logic and Reasoning:** Helping you weigh pros and cons before making decisions, seeing into the future.
- **Emotional Regulation:** Allowing you to manage strong emotions without immediately reacting.
- **Empathy:** Enabling you to understand and connect with others' feelings.
- **Self-Awareness:** Helping you reflect on your thoughts, behaviors, and goals.

When your PFC is in charge, you feel calm, composed, and capable of making thoughtful decisions. Whether you're resolving a conflict at work, planning for the future, or navigating a challenging conversation with a loved one, this part of your brain ensures you stay in control. But here's the catch: the PFC isn't always in charge. It can be easily hijacked by another, more primitive part of the brain—the amygdala.

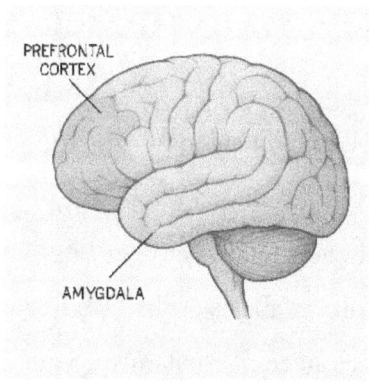

THE AMYGDALA: YOUR INTERNAL SECURITY GUARD

The amygdala's job is simple but essential: *to keep you alive.* Located deep within your brain, the amygdala is part of the limbic system, which governs emotions and survival instincts. If the PFC is the calm and collected CEO, the amygdala is the hyper-vigilant security guard, always on the lookout for danger.

The main role of the amygdala is to detect threats and trigger your body's *fight, flight, or freeze* response. This response was crucial for our ancestors, who needed to react quickly when faced with real physical dangers, like a charging predator. Even today, this response can be life-saving. For example, when you slam on the brakes to avoid a car accident, you can thank the amygdala for doing its job. In moments like this, the amygdala acts faster than the PFC, sending a surge of stress chemicals (like adrenaline) through your body to help you react quickly.

WHY THE AMYGDALA HIJACKS YOUR BRAIN

While the amygdala's rapid response is helpful in life-or-death situations, it can become problematic in modern life, particularly when it perceives a non-life-threatening event—like public speaking, a breakup, or a critical comment from your boss—as a major danger. In these moments, the amygdala reacts by flooding your system with the same stress hormones needed to slam on your brakes before a car accident. By doing so, this chemical release prohibits access to your PFC, making it harder for you to think clearly or respond rationally.

Here's another example: Have you ever been in an argument and said something hurtful in the heat of the moment, only to regret it later? That's the *security guard* in action. Once it senses a perceived threat (in this case, emotional pain or rejection), it overrides your logical brain and puts you in survival mode, sometimes causing you to say or do things you may regret after the escalation passes.

Later, when the PFC has regained control and you're wondering, *Why did I say that?...* You can blame it on the amygdala.

STRESS AND ITS TRIGGERS: WHEN THE AMYGDALA SOUNDS THE ALARM

The amygdala isn't picky about what it perceives as a threat. Its job is to react quickly, often before your logical brain (the PFC) has had a chance to assess whether the situation is truly dangerous. This means that both real threats (like physical danger) and perceived threats (like social rejection or failure) can activate the same *fight, flight, or freeze,* reflexes. Great for close calls in traffic, but not so great for everyday challenges that require a wise response.

Your brain responds to imagined threats the same way it responds to real ones. When you imagine a stressful scenario, your amygdala activates as though the threat is happening in real time, sending signals to your body to prepare for action. This means that simply *thinking* about a stressful situation—like an upcoming presentation or an awkward past social interaction—can trigger the same *fight, flight, or freeze* response as being physically threatened. Your heart might begin to race or your palms might sweat, even if you are safe in bed trying to fall asleep while imagining the stressful situation.

Let's take a closer look at some common life events that can trigger the amygdala's alarm system:

- **Breakups:** The end of a relationship can feel like the loss of safety and belonging, which the brain interprets as a major threat.
- **Fear of Abandonment:** Whether real or imagined, abandonment can trigger deep-rooted fears related to survival, as social connection has always been vital to human existence.
- **Rejection:** Our brains are wired to seek social acceptance. Rejection, whether romantic, professional, or personal, can set off the amygdala's alarm bells.
- **Failure:** Experiences of failure can trigger feelings of inadequacy and reinforce negative thought patterns.
- **Impostor Syndrome:** The fear of being "found out" as a fraud, despite evidence of your competence, can keep your amygdala on high alert.

- **Microaggressions and Discrimination:** Repeated experiences of subtle or overt discrimination can lead to chronic stress, keeping the amygdala in a prolonged state of vigilance.
- **Public Speaking**: For many of us, standing in front of an audience feels like being in the spotlight of potential judgment, which the brain interprets as a social threat.
- **Performance Demands:** Whether it's meeting a deadline at work or preparing for an exam, the pressure to perform can activate stress responses.
- **Loss or Grief:** The death of a loved one or any significant loss can trigger prolonged activation of the brain's stress system.

This list isn't exhaustive, but it highlights how everyday experiences—especially those involving social interaction and self-worth—can keep your brain's alarm system on repeat.

NEGATIVITY BIAS: WHY YOUR BRAIN FOCUSES ON THE BAD

Another evolutionary quirk that shapes how we experience stress is called *negativity bias*. This describes the brain's tendency to give more attention to negative experiences than positive ones. Why does this happen? Because in the context of survival, negative information was more important. Failing to notice a potential threat, like a lion, could be fatal, while missing out on something positive, like a cute rabbit, wasn't nearly as dangerous.

Even today, negativity bias plays a major role in how we perceive and process information. You might receive ten compliments in a day, but it's the one critical comment that sticks with you. That's negativity bias at work—your brain is hardwired to prioritize potential threats over positive experiences.

While this bias once helped humans survive, it can make life unnecessarily stressful in modern times. Constantly focusing on what's wrong can lead to rumination (replaying negative events in your mind) and anxiety (anticipating future problems).

NEURONS: YOUR BRAIN'S MESSENGERS

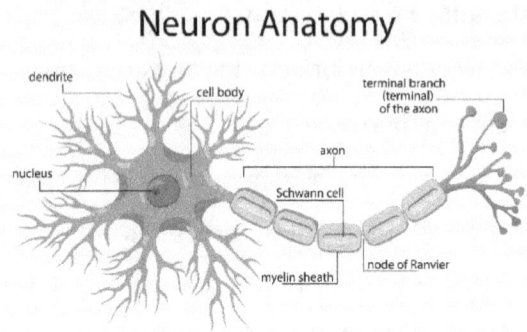

Now that we've discussed the prefrontal cortex (PFC)—the part responsible for rational thinking, planning, and self-control—and the amygdala—the emotional alarm system that detects threats—let's explore how they communicate together.

This is where neurons come in. Your brain is made up of approximately 86 billion neurons, which are specialized cells responsible for transmitting information between the PFC and amygdala, as well as all other parts of the brain. Neurons communicate with each other through electrical signals and chemical messengers called neurotransmitters. Over time, the more neurons that fire together, the stronger their connection becomes.

This is why neuroscientists often say,

> **"Neurons that fire together, wire together."**

Neurons connect to each other to form networks of neural pathways that pass on electrical impulses and information throughout the brain and body.

NEUROTRANSMITTERS: THE BRAIN'S CHEMICAL MESSENGERS

While neurons form the physical pathways in your brain, neurotransmitters are the chemicals that carry messages along those pathways. Different neurotransmitters have different effects on your mood, energy, and overall well-being. Some promote calm and happiness, while others trigger alertness and action.

In the coming chapters, there are a few key neurotransmitters we're going to focus on:

- **Dopamine**: Known as the "reward" chemical, dopamine plays a central role in motivation and pleasure. When you achieve something—whether it's completing a task or earning a compliment—your brain releases dopamine, creating positive feelings and encouraging you to seek out similar experiences.
- **Serotonin:** Often called the "mood stabilizer," serotonin helps regulate your mood, sleep, and appetite. Low levels of serotonin are linked to feelings of depression and anxiety, which is why many antidepressant medications work by increasing serotonin availability in the brain.
- **Oxytocin:** Known as the "love hormone," oxytocin promotes feelings of trust and connection. It's released during moments of bonding, like hugging a loved one or spending time with a pet, and it helps reduce stress by activating the parasympathetic nervous system.

- **Endorphins:** These are your body's "natural painkillers." They're released during physical activity, laughter, and moments of joy, helping to reduce pain and increase pleasure.
- **Cortisol**: Often referred to as the "stress hormone," cortisol is released by the adrenal glands during times of strain. Its primary role is to help the body manage energy by increasing blood sugar levels, suppressing non-essential processes like digestion, and supporting the *fight, flight, or freeze* response. Prolonged high levels of cortisol, however, can lead to issues like anxiety, poor sleep, and weight gain.
- **Adrenaline (Epinephrine):** This is the body's immediate response chemical, released during moments of acute stress. Adrenaline causes a surge in heart rate, increases blood flow to muscles, and sharpens focus, preparing the body to respond quickly to danger. While helpful in short bursts, frequent adrenaline spikes can lead to exhaustion and cardiovascular strain.

Each of these neurotransmitters plays an integral part in emotional regulation, which is why many of the techniques we're going to develop—like practicing gratitude, engaging in physical movement, and fostering connection—are designed to keep them balanced.

THE HABIT LOOP

Every time you think a thought, take an action, or experience an emotion, you're reinforcing a specific neural pathway. Over time, these repeated patterns become habits—both good and bad. Our brains are habit making machines. Going on autopilot helps free up space for the brain to process and function at max capacity.

For example, if you frequently respond to stress by overthinking or shutting down, those neural pathways become well-worn trails in your brain, making it easier for you to fall into those patterns again in the future.

But here's the encouraging part:

> **Just as negative habits can be wired in, positive habits can be wired in too.**

By intentionally practicing healthier responses—like pausing to breathe when you feel overwhelmed—you can create new neural pathways that make those healthy behaviors your brain's default response.

OVERACTIVATION OF THE AMYGDALA: THE COST OF CHRONIC STRESS

We've all been there at certain times in our lives: overwhelmed and over-stressed in habit loops. Both internal and external stressors can keep the amygdala in a state of overactivation, which comes with significant costs to both your mental and physical health.

When the *security guard* is working overtime your body stays in *fight, flight, or freeze* mode, flooding your system with stress hormones like adrenaline and cortisol.

While this response is useful in short bursts—like when you need to escape danger or wake up for that 6 am alarm—it becomes harmful when sustained over time. This creates a cascade of potentially harmful conditions in your brain.

REDUCED ACCESS TO THE PREFRONTAL CORTEX

When the amygdala is activated constantly, stress chemicals block us from accessing our PFC. This is why you might find it difficult to think clearly, make decisions, or regulate your emotions during stressful situations. You may notice shut down, procrastination or overwhelm as common responses to constant stress.

You may notice:

1. **Heightened Emotional Reactivity**

   An overactive amygdala makes you more prone to react emotionally rather than rationally. Small stressors that wouldn't normally bother you can feel overwhelming when your amygdala is on overdrive.

2. **Physical Health Consequences**

   Chronic stress doesn't just affect your mind—it impacts your body too. Prolonged activation of the *fight, flight, or freeze* response can lead to issues like high blood pressure, weakened immune function, and digestive problems. You might notice symptoms like frequent headaches, stomach aches, muscle tension, or fatigue when your stress levels are high.

3. **Negative Thought Patterns**

   When the brain is stuck in a stress loop, negative thought patterns are reinforced. Remember: *Neurons that fire together, wire together.* The more you focus on negative thoughts, the stronger those neural pathways become, making it easier for your brain to default to those thoughts in the future.

STRENGTHENING THE PFC, CALMING THE AMYGDALA

The ability of your brain to form new neural connections is known as: **neuroplasticity.**

Your brain isn't fixed—remember, it's constantly changing and adapting based on what you experience, and importantly, what you focus on. This is a game-changer! It means you have the power to reshape your brain through intentional practice and mindfulness around what you choose to focus in on.

More good news is that you don't have to sit back and let the amygdala take over whenever it offers to help. It's actually possible to train your brain to help keep the prefrontal *CEO* in control more often.

Just as you can strengthen a muscle through exercise, you can strengthen your PFC through practices like mindfulness, reflection, and emotional regulation techniques. At the same time, you can learn to calm your amygdala by recognizing its triggers and using specific tools to deactivate the *fight, flight, or freeze* response.

We made it—great work absorbing this complex chapter on neuroscience! The brain's structure and functioning patterns put us all on the same page—you are not alone with your mental health symptoms. Now understanding the basic foundation of how our brains work, we can dive into managing and regulating it.

SELF-REFLECTION WORKSHEET

What areas of your life bring you the most stress?

What triggers your amygdala the most?

Which stressors do you want to work on decreasing?

What new neural pathways and thought habits do you want to increase?

CHAPTER 1 CHEAT SHEET: BRAIN NEUROSCIENCE 101

- The prefrontal cortex helps with logical thinking, decision-making, and emotional regulation. Strengthening it allows you to stay calm and clear-headed.

- The amygdala is your brain's alarm system, responsible for triggering the *fight, flight, or freeze* response. Learning how to calm it down is key to managing stress.

- Neurons and neurotransmitters play a critical role in habit formation. Repeated behaviors strengthen neural pathways, which is why consistency matters in rewiring your brain.

- Your brain is wired for negativity bias, but you can counteract it by focusing on positive experiences and intentional skills.

- We want to strengthen the PFC (your calm and collected CEO) by building new neural pathways.

- We are trying to decrease overactivation and excess wiring of neurons from the amygdala's *fight, flight, or freeze* impacting the rest of the system.

- What we focus on grows neurobiologically. Neurons that fire together, wire together.

Chapter 2: Mindful Awareness

What is Mindful Awareness?

- The quality or state of being conscious or aware of something.
- A mental state achieved by focusing one's awareness on the present moment, while calmly acknowledging and accepting one's feelings, thoughts, and bodily sensations, used as a therapeutic technique.
- "The awareness that arises from paying attention, on purpose, in the present moment and non-judgmentally." ~Kabat-Zinn

Imagine you're standing on the edge of a stream, watching colorful Fall leaves float by. The leaves represent your thoughts—each one rushing in a different direction. Some are worries, others are regrets, and others could be hopes and dreams for the future.

Now imagine you have two choices: You can either jump into the stream, trying to control and direct the flow of each leaf, or you can stand still and simply observe without getting tangled up in it.

That act of standing still and observing without interference? That's mindfulness.

Mindfulness, in its simplest form, is the practice of paying attention to the present moment, without judgment or resistance. It's about noticing your thoughts and emotions as they arise but not letting them carry you away.

The modern definition comes from Jon Kabat-Zinn, who describes mindfulness as:

> **"The awareness that arises from paying attention, on purpose, in the present moment, and non-judgmentally."**

In other words, it's about consciously tuning in to what's happening right now, whether that's a sensation in your body, a sound in your environment, or a thought crossing your mind.

Mindfulness is about intentional awareness, as opposed to habits and routines that are stuck on autopilot. Mindfulness is about being present.

Most of the time we can be physically in one place but mentally somewhere else—replaying yesterday's conversations, worrying about tomorrow's deadlines, or zoning out in front of a screen. This constant mental time-traveling fuels stress, anxiety, and a sense of disconnection from ourselves and the world around us.

Based on the foundational knowledge we gained from chapter one, not being present can add to the constant triggering of our *fight, flight, or freeze* system, but mindfulness can offer us a way to strengthen our PFC, calm the amygdala and reduce chronic stress hormones and symptoms.

Science has shown us many benefits of practicing mindful

awareness. Brain studies have demonstrated that these habits actually grow gray matter in the self-confident and emotionally regulating parts of the brain—the same region of the brain where meditation strength is built.

With all of these benefits, it's no wonder the initial phase of most counseling treatments is getting to know your *mindful observer*, noticing all the racing thoughts and emotions in order to identify what needs to be worked on. (We'll talk about the *mindful observer* more in our first exercise below.) Mindful awareness of what our brains are thinking is one of the most important skills to practice in short term therapy. **Why? Because we cannot change what we are not aware of.**

In essence, mindfulness gives you a mental pause button. Instead of reacting automatically to every stressful situation, **you can learn to create a space between stimulus and response**. This space is where your power lies—the power to choose how you want to respond, rather than being controlled by racing thoughts and emotions.

HOW TO PRACTICE MINDFUL AWARENESS

Mindful awareness of what is happening in the present can be done in any activity, in any moment.

There are two main ways to practice mindfulness: Formal meditation and informal daily moments of awareness.

- **Formal Meditation:** This involves setting aside a specific time to sit quietly and focus on something like your breath, a sound, or a sensation. When your mind inevitably wanders, you gently bring your attention back to the present moment. Over time, this practice trains your brain to stay focused and calm.

- **Informal Daily Moments of Awareness:** This is *anytime, anywhere* mindfulness you can practice simply by bringing conscious awareness to everyday activities—whether you're brushing your teeth, eating a meal, or walking outside. These moments, though small, add up and help reinforce the habit of staying present.

In other words, you don't necessarily have to sit for 30 minutes a day, legs crossed, chanting *Om* to reap the life-changing benefits of mindfulness! You can start right now with simple steps in connection with things you're already doing. Throughout the rest of this chapter, we'll focus on just that—growing your amazing mindfulness muscle through easy, manageable daily exercises you can attach to your normal habits, like brushing your teeth or falling asleep.

Our first exercise, however, will take just a few minutes of quiet focus to lay the groundwork for more on-the-go techniques.

It's time for you to meet your *mindful observer*.

BECOMING THE MINDFUL OBSERVER

We are not our thoughts. **We are the awareness capable of observing those thoughts.**

This distinction is crucial, because it means you don't have to identify with every passing thought or emotion. Feeling anxious doesn't mean you are an anxious person. Having a negative thought doesn't define you as a negative thinker.

That awareness—the part of you that can step back and watch your thoughts and emotions without getting swept away by them—is called your **mindful observer**, one of the core concepts of mindfulness we'll be building on as you progress.

By cultivating the *mindful observer*, you can create a space to acknowledge inner experiences without being defined by them.

Over time, you'll discover that your *mindful observer* can be ever-present, helping control what you focus on and when.

Our first exercise is all about introducing the *mindful observer* into your daily life. This powerful visualization—and example of formal meditation—will put you on the path to mastering thousands of daily thoughts and ever-changing emotions. It will be an important foundation for the more bite-size techniques you'll soon develop. So put aside 5-10 minutes of distraction-free time, any time of the day, in a comfortable, safe place—and let's dive in!

VISUALIZATION: SKY, SUN, AND WEATHER

- **Mindfulness as the sky:** Take a few deep breathes and feel free to close your eyes. Bring to mind a picture of the sky—always present, vast, and holding space for weather patterns (thoughts/emotions) that pass through it. Storms come, clouds gather, and eventually, they drift away. But the sky remains. That's your mindful awareness — the vast space that can observe your thoughts and emotions without getting swept away by them. Stay here for a few minutes, observing and sensing all the aspects of the large, blue sky in our mind. Non-judgmentally notice which thoughts and sensations are emerging within your sky space. If you get pulled into specific thought spirals, gently notice it and bring your focus back into the embodiment of the sky space, differentiated away from the constant passing thoughts. What do you notice? What do you feel emerging within your sky?

- **Authentic Confidence as the sun:** Now that you've spent some time connecting with your *mindful observer* as the sky, take a few minutes to focus in on what a sun would look like in your visualization. This sun can represent your Authentic Confident Self (abbreviated as the "ACS"- which we will dive into deeper in upcoming chapters). This is the part of you that does not disappear even when life gets tough and dark clouds move in. Like the sun, it's always there, representing your strengths, values and power to regulate. Confidence-building is about learning to trust that the sun will shine again, no matter how thick the clouds may seem. How does your sun feel internally? Which characteristics are you proud of that the sun represents? Stay here for as long as you need, observing the uniqueness of your own sun and what strengths it represents within you.

- **Thoughts and Emotions as weather**: Now begin to shift your attention to the common thoughts and emotions that may take up space in your sky and cloud your sun. Passing thoughts and emotions, like weather, are temporary but can be impactful if we ignore them. They change, come and go, and sometimes catch us off guard. But just as you wouldn't let a rainy day define your entire week, you don't have to let a passing thought define your whole identity.

What are the categories of ruminations in your weather patterns? How often do they cloud your sun? Calmly hold space for whatever weather comes and goes. You don't need to fight the storms or cling to the sunshine. Just be the sky, observing it all. Stay here for as many minutes as needed, absorbing and being present with this internal visualization.

This exercise reinforces the idea that emotions are temporary—they come and go like the weather. But your mindful awareness, like the sky, remains constant.

The more you practice this, the easier it becomes to detach from emotional storms and return to a place of calm observation.

WHY VISUALIZATION WORKS

You might be wondering, "How can imagining something like the sky or the sun actually help me manage my emotions?" The answer lies in how the brain processes mental imagery. Neuroscientific research has shown that visualization activates the same neural pathways as real experiences. When you imagine a calming image, like a vast blue sky, your brain responds as if you're actually seeing it, triggering a relaxation response in your body.

Visualization also helps interrupt negative thought patterns. When you're caught in a loop of anxiety or overthinking, introducing a mental image gives your mind something else to focus on, breaking the cycle and creating space for more mindful awareness. Long-term meditators—those who have practiced mindfulness consistently over several years—show significant changes in their brain structure.

Specifically, they have increased gray matter density in the PFC and decreased activity in the amygdala.

DAILY MINDFULNESS PRACTICES

Great job completing your first visualization exercise! If you got distracted or had a hard time focusing, *don't worry*. Like any new skill, mindfulness can feel unfamiliar at first — even a bit frustrating with racing thoughts popping in and out of your mind. A little distraction and discouragement are normal.

Remember, your brain took decades to wire itself before you picked up this book, so patience and practice to rewire new skills might also take some time. Keep going and keep practicing! The more consistently you practice, the more natural it will begin to feel. Over time, it can become second nature.

Now that you've got a sense of how your *mindful observer* can help you step back from changing thoughts and emotions and stay present, you're ready to try some more in-the-moment applications. While the *Sky, Sun, and Weather* visualization offers a deeper, more immersive experience, it can also be helpful to:

> Reinforce your mindfulness habit with quick, accessible practices woven into your daily routine.

These brief moments of awareness can make an additional, helpful impact.

Think of the following exercises as mini, informal mental workouts — each one offering a chance to strengthen your mindful observer and retrain your brain to stay grounded in just a few minutes each day.

TOOTHBRUSHING EXERCISE

This might sound like a strange place to practice mindfulness, but it can be a perfect pairing as it is something we do every day. Normally, when brushing your teeth, your mind is likely wandering—thinking about what's ahead for the day or ruminating on something that happened yesterday. This exercise helps you anchor your attention in the present moment to start developing the 'mindfulness muscle' and instantly bringing your PFC on board.

How it works:

- As you begin brushing your teeth, shift your focus to the sensations involved.
- Notice the taste of the toothpaste, the feel of the bristles on your teeth, and the temperature of the water.
- If your mind starts to wander (which it will), gently bring your attention back to these sensations.
- Focus in on any internal sensations of the activity, and over and over again when thought patterns pop up, notice them and refocus.
- No judgment—just awareness. The goal isn't to force your mind to stay focused perfectly but to practice bringing it back whenever it drifts.

Why it works: This exercise turns a mundane, automatic activity into a moment of conscious awareness. Over time, this habit will train your brain to be more present during other parts of your day as well.

WHAT AM I THINKING RIGHT NOW? (POP QUIZ EXERCISE)

Throughout the day, your mind produces an endless stream of thoughts—some helpful, many not. This exercise helps you become aware of those thought patterns by checking in with yourself regularly.

How it works:

- Set a reminder on your phone or a mental cue (for example, *every time I sit down*) to ask yourself, "What am I thinking right now?"
- Pause and observe your current thoughts without judgment. Are they positive? Uncomfortable? Neutral? Racing, quiet, humorous?
- Simply label the thoughts (e.g., planning, worrying, replaying the past) and bring your attention back to the present.

Why it works: Often, we're so caught up in our thoughts that we don't even realize what's occupying our mind. This exercise helps you break that automatic loop by increasing your awareness of your thinking patterns. Once you're aware, you can choose whether to engage with those thoughts or let them pass.

FALLING ASLEEP EXERCISE

Nighttime can be one of the hardest times to quiet your mind. Racing thoughts often surface when the distractions of the day fade away, making it difficult to fall asleep. This exercise helps you shift from being lost in thought to being grounded in the present moment.

How it works:

- As you lie in bed, bring your attention to the physical sensations of lying down—notice the weight of your body against the mattress, the feel of the sheets, and the rhythm of your breathing.
- If your mind starts racing with worries or replaying the day's events, gently guide your focus back to those sensations in the body.
- You can also try silently repeating a calming word or phrase, like "relax" or "peace," with each breath.

Why it works: This exercise helps calm the nervous system by anchoring your attention in your body rather than your thoughts. Over time, it can improve sleep quality by reducing nighttime overthinking.

SAVORING FOOD EXERCISE

Eating is another daily activity we often do mindlessly — rushing through meals while scrolling on our phones or thinking about our to-do lists. This exercise invites you to slow down and fully experience your food, turning an ordinary meal into an act of mindfulness.

How it works:

- Before you take your first bite, pause and take a moment to look at your food. Notice the colors, textures, and smells.
- As you begin eating, focus on the taste and texture of each bite. How does the flavor change as you chew? What sensations do you notice in your mouth?
- If your mind starts to wander, gently bring your attention back to the experience of eating.

Why it works: This practice not only helps cultivate mindfulness but also enhances your enjoyment of food. It can also promote healthier eating habits by helping you tune in to your body's hunger and fullness cues. Savoring through our senses can be a positive experience, pulling us into a calm and regulated present focus.

SAVORING NATURE EXERCISE

Whether you're walking in the park, sitting by a lake, or simply noticing the trees outside your window, there's something inherently calming about being in nature. This exercise helps you deepen that connection by pairing it with mindful observation.

How it works:

- Choose a time each day to spend a few minutes outside.
- As you walk or sit, bring your attention to the sights, sounds, and smells around you. Notice the rustling of leaves, the warmth of the sun on your skin, or the sound of birds in the distance. Notice how all five senses engage with the wonderous world of nature around you.
- Whenever your mind starts to wander, gently bring your focus back to the natural environment.

Why it works: Nature has a grounding effect on the mind, helping to reduce stress and improve mood. By practicing mindfulness in nature, you're also reinforcing your ability to stay present in other situations.

MINDFUL DRIVING EXERCISE

Driving is another activity where our minds often wander on autopilot. This exercise helps you stay present during your commute, transforming what might normally be a stressful or monotonous experience into a moment of mindfulness.

How it works:

- As you start your drive, take a moment to tune in to your body—notice how your hands feel on the steering wheel and how your feet feel on the pedals. Scan your body internally noticing the sensations, as well as externally in your driving space.
- As the drive continues, continue to bring your attention to what you see, hear, and feel—the passing scenery, the sound of the engine, or the sensation of the car moving beneath you.
- If your mind starts to drift into planning or worrying, gently bring your focus back to the present moment.

Why it works: This exercise not only cultivates mindfulness but also promotes safer driving by keeping your attention on the road. Tuning in to structures, roads, and trees you may have completely missed on your previous commutes can help bring you into the present.

TURNING ORDINARY MOMENTS INTO MINDFUL OPPORTUNITIES

Already, in reading through this chapter, you have given yourself a great list of mindfulness practices to choose from! However, with busy schedules, commitments, and life responsibilities, it can be overwhelming to add one more thing to our endless to-do lists.

Another tool you can use to seamlessly integrate these practices into our lives is pairing informal mindfulness moments with boring, inevitable parts of our day. These exercises can help us build the mindfulness habit quickly and naturally without scheduling it.

For example, I used to notice that whenever I was waiting for a client to check into a therapy session, I experienced anxiety about whether they would show up. Over time, I started to pair these few minutes of anxious time with mindfulness practices, transforming a moment of dread into a moment of focus and growth. Below are a variety of ideas on how to transform mundane daily moments into mindfulness growth opportunities.

MINDFUL WAITING

We spend a surprising amount of time waiting—waiting in line, waiting for an elevator, waiting for a webpage to load. Instead of reaching for your phone or letting impatience take over, use these moments as an opportunity to practice mindfulness.

How it works:

- As you find yourself waiting, bring your attention to your breath. Notice the rise and fall of your chest with each inhale and exhale. Notice the sensation of air leaving each nostril and your mouth.
- If your mind starts to wander, gently guide it back to the sensation of breathing.
- You can also take a moment to notice your surroundings—the sounds, sights, and smells around you. Ground yourself in your five senses and pull your focus away from impatience.

Why it works: Mindful waiting helps turn what might otherwise feel like wasted time into a moment of calm presence. It also reduces impatience by shifting your focus from what you can't control (the wait) to what you can (your breath and awareness).

MINDFUL LISTENING

We often listen to respond, not to truly hear. This exercise helps you practice listening with full attention, without jumping in to offer advice, interrupt, or build your response.

How it works:

- The next time you're in a conversation, try to listen fully to the other person. Pay attention to their words, tone, and body language.
- Resist the urge to plan your response while they're speaking. Instead, focus entirely on understanding what they're saying.
- Notice the pauses, and spaces in between the words and sentences.
- When it's your turn to speak, take a moment to pause before responding.

Why it works: Mindful listening deepens your connection with others and helps you stay present in conversations. It also reduces misunderstandings and enhances empathy.

MINDFUL STRETCHING

Whether you're sitting at a desk all day or feeling tense after any long endeavor, mindful stretching is a great way to combine movement with awareness.

How it works:

- Choose a simple stretch, like reaching your arms overhead or gently twisting your torso.
- As you stretch, bring your attention to the sensations in your body — the feeling of your muscles lengthening, the stretch in your spine, the contact of your feet with the floor.
- Move slowly and mindfully, paying attention to your breath as you stretch.

Why it works: Mindful stretching not only helps release physical tension but also anchors your mind in the present moment. It's a great way to reset your focus during a busy day.

These daily mindfulness practices may seem small, but their impact is cumulative.

> **Each time you bring your attention back to the present moment, you're rewiring your brain, strengthening your PFC, and calming your amygdala.**

Think of every mindful moment as a mental push-up—over time, these tiny efforts add up, making it easier to stay present and balanced throughout your day. You can start by practicing these tools a few times a day, reminding yourself through Post-It notes or phone alarms. Over time, like reps at the gym, increase your frequency when you feel ready and comfortable. Noticing the times of day where you feel the most triggered can also be a neon sign pointing to where mindfulness tools could be most helpful.

CULTIVATING SELF-COMPASSION THROUGH MINDFUL AWARENESS

We are already well on the way toward mastering mindfulness, and now we're on the home stretch! So far, we've filled our toolkit with longer visualizations, mini-workouts to practice throughout the day, and informal moments to integrate mindfulness practices *wherever* and *whenever* we find ourselves.

The final skill set we will cover is integrating self-compassion into your practice. As you deepen your mindfulness practice, you'll inevitably encounter moments when self-judgment sneaks in. You might catch yourself thinking, "I shouldn't be feeling this way," or

"Why can't I stay calm like everyone else?" This is where self-compassion becomes essential.

> **Mindful awareness isn't just about observing your thoughts and emotions—it's also about approaching them with kindness and non-judgement.**

Without self-compassion, mindfulness can turn into another way to criticize yourself for not being "better" at handling life's stressors.

Self-compassion is the ability to treat yourself with the same kindness, care, and understanding that you would offer a best friend. Imagine if a friend came to you feeling overwhelmed and anxious. Would you tell them they were crazy or overreacting? Of course not. You'd probably offer reassurance, a listening ear, and maybe even a few words of encouragement. Yet, when it comes to our own struggles, we often default to harsh self-criticism. Our shared goals will be defining self-compassion, and integrating it into our mindfulness activities.

THE THREE ELEMENTS OF SELF-COMPASSION

According to Dr. Kristin Neff, a leading researcher on self-compassion, there are three key elements to practicing self-compassion:

1. **Mindfulness**

   You can't be compassionate toward yourself if you're unaware of what's happening inside. Mindfulness, like we've discussed, allows you to notice your suffering without exaggerating it or suppressing it. It's about acknowledging your pain with openness and curiosity.

2. **Common Humanity**

   One of the most isolating aspects of difficult emotions is the feeling that you're alone in your struggle. Self-compassion reminds you that suffering is part of the shared human experience. You are not alone! Everyone faces moments of fear, doubt, sadness, and frustration. You are not broken, or too much—you are human.

3. **Self-Kindness**

   This involves offering yourself warmth and understanding when you're going through a tough time. Instead of beating yourself up for feeling anxious or sad, self-kindness invites you to respond with care. It's about replacing the inner critic with a supportive inner voice, just like you would offer to a best friend.

A MINDFUL SELF-COMPASSION EXERCISE

In addition to the formal and informal mindfulness workouts we've already covered, the following skill will be useful whenever you're feeling overwhelmed or caught in self-judgment:

1. **Pause and take a deep breath.**

   Close your eyes if that feels comfortable, and bring your attention to your breath. Let the act of breathing anchor you in the present moment. Inhale for four counts, and exhale for four counts. Notice how the breath feels coming in and out of your body.

2. **Acknowledge what you're feeling.**

   Silently name the thoughts and emotions you are noticing internally: "This is anxiety," or "I'm feeling overwhelmed right now." Remember, the goal isn't to change how you feel—it's simply to acknowledge it with mindfulness.

3. **Remind yourself of common humanity.**

   Say to yourself, "Everyone feels this way sometimes. I'm not alone in this." This simple reminder can reduce feelings of isolation and help you connect to the shared human experience (while activating and strengthening your PFC).

4. **Offer yourself kindness.**

   Place a hand on your heart or another soothing spot, and say something supportive to yourself such as, "It's okay to feel this way, this too shall pass." or "We can solve this problem together." Choose words that feel natural and comforting in your space of present, non-judgmental mindfulness.

Practicing compassionate mindfulness can lead us to our greatest superpower: *self-awareness.* Whether we're struggling with anxiety, depression or insecurity, we cannot change what we don't see. Truly knowing our internal landscape with all its thoughts, behaviors and motivations can give us the key to lasting change.

SELF-REFLECTION WORKSHEET

To support your journey toward greater mindful self-awareness, take a moment to reflect on and complete the following prompts. They're designed to help you tune in, observe, and better understand your inner world.

Feelings breakdown: Which emotions do you notice internally?

✓ Check which ones you are feeling.

Sadness:

unhappy	gloomy	low
dejected	heartbroken	hopeless
regretful	melancholic	sullen
depressed	distressed	lonely
down	bored	apathetic
numb	bad	isolated

Worry:

nervous	tense	overwhelmed
scared	troubled	discouraged
apprehensive	agitated	helpless
hesitant	alarmed	confused
bothered	uncertain	
uptight	panicked	

Self-doubt:

shameful	insignificant	ashamed
guilty	inadequate	skeptical
rejected	embarrassed	critical
submissive	inferior	
insecure	stupid	

Anger:

hurt	jealous	livid
hostile	disconnected	vengeful
selfish	resentful	aggravated
frustrated	rageful	inpatient
discouraged	mad	
irritated	bitter	

What thoughts do I notice most throughout the day?

Are they positive, neutral, or uncomfortable? Do they tend to focus on a specific topic, like work or relationships?

What emotions do I experience most frequently?

Are there certain emotions that keep coming up throughout the day? How do I respond to those emotions?

Where do I notice my attention being pulled to?

Does my mind spend a lot of time in the past or future? Were there moments today when I was fully present?

What moments of mindfulness stood out to me today?

Were there times when I was able to pause, take a breath, and be present? How did that feel?

What would I like to do differently tomorrow?

Is there a specific situation where I'd like to bring more mindfulness or a pattern I'd like to be more aware of?

CHAPTER 2 CHEAT SHEET: MINDFUL AWARENESS

- Mindfulness is "the awareness that arises from paying attention, on purpose, in the present moment and non-judgmentally." ~ Jon Kabat-Zinn.
- Create a visualization of your mindful observer.
- Carve out specific times each day to practice.
- Identify and categorize your emotions and thought patterns through daily mindful observing.
- Mindfulness can be practiced at any time, anywhere.
- Observing and labelling your emotions and experiences helps strengthen your mindful observer and PFC at the same time.
- Being compassionate towards yourself internally is a key part of mindfulness.
- The more you practice, the more natural engaging the mindful observer will be.

Chapter 3: Authentic Confident Self

What is the Authentic Confidence Self?

- The core of your identity, which no one can change or take away from you.
- Your own strengths, values, and unique life purpose.
- The sense of who you are that flows without fear of judgment from others.
- Genuine, real, truthful, reliable, trustworthy part of self.

Years ago, I worked with a client named Janessa. She came to therapy paralyzed by symptoms of anxiety and depression. Her *fight, flight, or freeze* response was constantly on replay, making it almost impossible for her nervous system to rest. The fear and shutdown reflex was a habit her PFC could not overcome alone.

Janessa's psyche was bombarded daily with negative racing thoughts and emotions. However, through mindfulness and self-exploration, we went on an inward journey to uncover parts of her Authentic Confident Self (ACS) — a version of herself present since childhood, but masked by many layers of life's pain.

We discovered that as a child, Janessa had found great joy in sharing her talents of drawing and writing. Growing into emerging adulthood and having a child of her own, she had also developed a fierce passion and strength revolving around protecting and loving her new baby. Janessa's ACS began to materialize, composed of all her strengths, joys, talents, and maternal values. She even drew a picture of her ACS: a vibrant, strong, warrior-Queen created through her talented imagination.

Over time, Janessa learned to engage with thoughts and actions based on what her ACS would *choose*, not what the anxious and depressed voices demanded. The more we talked about and gave attention to her ACS, the stronger it became.

You too, like Janessa, have the power to access parts of yourself that may be hidden. Authentic confidence is more than just a feeling—it is an inherent part of our psyches that every human can have access to. It comes from knowing who you are, what you stand for, and trusting your ability to navigate life's challenges. Unlike false confidence, which relies on external factors like appearance, status, or achievements, our ACS can be found rooted in our inner world—comprising the values, strengths, and core of our individual identity. It's the unchangeable part of you that remains steady, no matter what storms you face.

When you entered this world, you didn't need anyone to tell you how to be confident. You explored, played, laughed, and expressed yourself freely. You didn't worry about whether you were good enough or if people approved of you. That innate confidence was simply part of your being, shining brightly like the sun on a clear day. But as life went on, experiences began to cloud that light.

In other words, over time, life can overshadow our ACS. Negative experiences—like criticism, failure, or rejection—create layers of self-doubt and insecurity. Social pressures and unrealistic expectations make us feel like we're not enough unless we meet certain standards. Slowly, we start to lose touch with who we are at our core.

But here's a truth: *your Authentic Confident Self is still there, waiting to be uncovered.* Beneath the layers of doubt and fear lies that same confident, joyful version of yourself who once savored the present freely without worry.

> **The key to accessing your ACS is reconnecting with your core strengths and values—the things that make you feel alive, inspired, and true to yourself.**

Authenticity is the new cool.

When you act in alignment with your authentic and unique design, you're able to connect with the life path that truly reflects your deepest desires — not the one imposed by societal standards or external pressure.

In a world of screens saturated with constant images of fame and wealth, it's easy to be conditioned into believing that our purpose must mirror the lives of celebrities or social media influencers. But when we chase someone else's version of success — fueled by fear, insecurity, or a sense of inadequacy — we disconnect from our own innate gifts, passions, and vision.

When our goals are driven by survival mode — by *fight, flight, or freeze* chemistry, self-judgment, or the need for validation — we end up running in circles, striving but never fully arriving. This keeps us from recognizing the unique blueprint that's already inside us.

The path to your true purpose can begin when you grow your internal magnet of self-worth — drawing you again and again into experiences, relationships, and opportunities that align with your ACS.

So pause and ask yourself: Who is your Authentic Confident Self? And what would your life look like if you followed that version of you every day?

REDISCOVERING YOUR ACS

Sometimes, when we've spent years clouded by anxious or depressive symptoms, it can feel hard to uncover our ACS. Thankfully, confidence can be strengthened through patterns—cultivated over time with consistent actions and intentional reflection. One of the most effective ways to activate and stay connected to your ACS is by creating:

A Personal Confidence Blueprint.

This blueprint will act as an internal guiding force, like Janessa's queen warrior visualization. Think of it as a roadmap that can remind you of who you are, what you stand for and what strengths you bring to this world.

Your confidence blueprint will include three key elements:

- Core Strengths
- Core Values
- Confidence Rituals

Our next step is to set aside a few minutes to identify each of these elements through the following reflections. Once we've defined our Core Strengths, Values, and Rituals, we'll be able to act and think in line with our most authentic self, no matter what challenges arise.

IDENTIFYING YOUR CORE STRENGTHS

Take a moment to reflect on the following questions. Write down whatever comes to mind—there are no right or wrong answers.

What did you love to do as a child?
Think back to activities that brought you joy before you started worrying about being good at them. Did you love drawing, storytelling, building things, or exploring nature?

What are your natural talents?
These might be things you're good at without much effort, such as problem-solving, making people laugh, or offering a listening ear.

What do people often compliment you on?

Sometimes others can see our strengths more clearly than we can. Think about the positive feedback you've received from friends, family, or colleagues.

What brings you a sense of purpose?

Are there activities or causes that make you feel deeply fulfilled, even if they're challenging?

What parts of your identity and culture are you proud of?

Are there rituals or community connections that help highlight your ancestral strengths and wisdom?

Once you've identified your core strengths, keep them somewhere visible—write them in a journal, post them on your mirror, or save them as a wallpaper on your phone. These strengths are like the rays of your inner sun, shining through even on cloudy days.

IDENTIFYING YOUR CORE VALUES

While strengths help you recognize what you're good at, value clarification can help guide how you live. They're the principles that matter most to you—the things that give your life meaning and purpose. Living in alignment with your values strengthens your sense of authenticity, which in turn fuels your confidence.

Take a moment to reflect on the following questions. Write down whatever comes to mind—remembering there are no right or wrong answers.

- **Reflect on past moments in which you have felt truly fulfilled.** What was happening in those moments? Were you helping others, creating something, learning something new?

- **Ask yourself: What's non-negotiable in my life?** These are the principles you're not willing to compromise on, even when it's inconvenient or difficult.

- **Choose five to ten values that feel most essential to you.** Examples might include integrity, creativity, kindness, courage, or growth.

- **If you were to write a personal statement on what your mission, purpose, and values are on this planet, what would it look like?**

Feeling stuck trying to uncover all the aspects of your ACS? You are not alone! Thankfully, Richard Swartz, the founder of Internal Family Systems Therapy, has created a simple guide to identifying qualities of our authentic self.

Below are 8 core states of being, all starting with the letter C, that emerge when we are connected with our ACS. Notice when and where these qualities emerge to connect deeper with your ACS:

Calmness: A state of being peaceful and grounded, even in the face of stress.

Clarity: The ability to see things clearly and objectively, without judgment.

Compassion: Feeling empathy and understanding towards oneself and others.

Confidence: Having faith in one's abilities and capacity to handle life's challenges.

Courage: The ability to face fears and uncertainties with resilience.

Connectedness: Feeling a sense of belonging and unity with oneself and others.

Creativity: The ability to find new solutions and express oneself in unique ways.

Curiosity: An openness to explore and learn new things, including one's own inner world.

IDENTIFYING CONFIDENCE RITUALS:

If you've spent some time working through the previous self-awareness prompts, you should be getting a deeper sense of what your strengths and values are. Confidence isn't something you build once and forget about, however—it's something we need to nurture daily. Confidence rituals are small, intentional habits that help you stay connected to your ACS. They don't have to be complicated or time-consuming, they just need to be consistent. We can start at self-acceptance and, with practice, work towards self-love over time. Below is a brief structure of how to engage with building our ACS daily:

1. **Give Yourself a Morning Boost**

   Visualization is a powerful tool for building confidence. Each morning, take a few minutes to visualize yourself succeeding in a situation where you want to feel more confident. Imagine yourself speaking clearly, feeling calm, and radiating self-assurance. Image what it would be like if your ACS led your thoughts and choices through the day. The more vividly you can imagine it, the more your brain will start to associate that situation with confidence rather than fear.

   Start your day with a simple confidence-boosting routine. This might include:

   - Repeat your strengths and values out loud or in your mind.
   - Visualize a successful day ahead, picturing yourself navigating challenges with calm and confidence.

- Write down one thing you're grateful for and one strength you plan to use that day.

  This practice sets a positive tone for the day, reminding you of your strengths and reinforcing your ability to handle whatever comes your way.

2. **Give Yourself a Positive Midday Check-In**

We all have an inner dialogue running through our minds throughout the day. For many of us, this dialogue tends to be more critical than supportive. Positive self-talk involves consciously replacing negative thoughts with encouraging ones.

Around midday, take a few minutes to pause and check in with yourself:

- How am I feeling right now?
- Which strengths have I brought forward today?
- How can I bring my values into the rest of my day?

This quick check-in helps you stay mindful of your actions and reinforces your confidence by focusing on what's going well.

3. **Finish Up with a Positive Evening Reflection**

Each evening, take a few minutes to reflect on your day and write down three things you did well. These don't have to be big accomplishments—small wins count too.

Maybe you completed a task at work, had a meaningful conversation, or took care of yourself in some way. The goal is to train your brain to focus on your strengths rather than your shortcomings.

- What went well today?

- What is one situation that you handled better than before?
- What was one thing you were proud of today?

This practice helps train your brain to focus on your strengths and progress, rather than on what went wrong or what you didn't achieve.

PUTTING IT ALL TOGETHER: YOUR CONFIDENCE BLUEPRINT

You've made it this far — give yourself a boost of confidence for that — Cheers! Now that we have identified three key elements of ACS—Core Strengths, Core Values, and Confidence Rituals—it's time to put them together into a personal confidence blueprint.

This is your unique design — a creative, empowering expression of your Authentic Confident Self. There's no right or wrong way to build it.

> **Feel free to use whatever medium speaks to you.**

- Create a dedicated page in your journal or a digital document.
- Write down each section clearly. Include your core strengths, values, a list of empowering beliefs, and a few confidence rituals you plan to practice daily.
- Keep your blueprint visible. Whether it's on your desk, your phone, or your bathroom mirror, having your blueprint in a place you'll see

regularly will remind you to stay aligned with your authentic self.

- Create a character that represents your internal ACS with visual forms if words become overwhelming.
- Review and update your blueprint regularly. As you grow and evolve, so will your strengths, values, and beliefs. Make it a habit to review your blueprint every few months and update it as needed.

PROTECTING YOUR CONFIDENCE FROM NEGATIVE INFLUENCES

Now that we have identified—and strengthened—our internal ACS, it is important to be on the lookout for the number one confidence sabotage: *negativity*.

Confidence can be fragile when exposed to negativity—whether from toxic relationships, unsupportive environments, or the constant comparison trap of social media. Protecting your confidence requires setting boundaries and curating a positive mental environment. A simplified way to stay in your ACS and battle negativity? *Set boundaries* and *let go of the comparison trap*.

1. **Setting Boundaries with Others**

    Some people, intentionally or unintentionally, bring negativity into our lives. They might criticize, belittle, or undermine our achievements. While you can't control others' behavior, you can control how much access they have to your inner world.

    Here are a few guiding principles on how to set boundaries:

    - *Identify the behaviors that impact your confidence.* For example, do you have a friend who constantly makes backhanded compliments or a colleague who dismisses your ideas? Recognizing these patterns can be the first step towards changing them.

    - *Communicate your boundaries clearly.* Use "I" statements to express your needs, e.g., "I feel disrespected when my ideas are dismissed. I'd appreciate it if we could have a more open dialogue."

- *Enforce your boundaries.* If someone continues to disregard your boundaries, it's okay to limit your interactions with them. Protecting your mental and emotional well-being is not selfish—it's necessary.

2. Navigating the Comparison Trap

Social media and societal expectations can often tempt us to compare our lives to others'. But comparison is a confidence killer—it shifts your focus from your own journey to someone else's highlight reel. Remember, everyone's path is different, and what you see online rarely reflects the full picture.

Here's how to avoid the comparison trap:

- *Limit your time on social media.* Set boundaries for how often you check your feeds and unfollow accounts that trigger feelings of inadequacy. Try to follow accounts that inspire you or bring you joy.

- *Celebrate your own milestones.* Instead of focusing on what others have achieved, reflect on your progress and accomplishments. Keep your eye on your own journey, not others!

- *Practice gratitude.* When you focus on what you have rather than what you lack, it's easier to feel content and confident in your own life.

Your confidence, like the sun, is always there, even when hidden behind life's challenges. By practicing mindfulness, reframing doubt, and nurturing your ACS, you can strengthen your confidence and carry it with you through every storm. Remember, confidence isn't about perfection—it's about showing up, staying true to yourself, and trusting that you're enough, just as you are.

CONFIDENCE AS A PRACTICE, NOT A DESTINATION

Just like building physical strength requires regular exercise, building authentic confidence requires consistent effort. Some days, your confidence might feel strong and unshakable. Other days, it might feel distant or hidden behind layers of doubt. Impostor Syndrome is something we all have dealt with at some point in our lives. That's okay. The goal isn't to feel confident all the time—it's to keep practicing, even when it's hard.

Think of confidence as a muscle. The more you practice using it, the stronger it becomes. And just like with any muscle, you don't have to start with heavy lifting. Small, consistent actions—like speaking up in a meeting, trying something new, or setting a healthy boundary—help build your confidence over time. Celebrate your ACS and how far you have come!

SELF-REFLECTION WORKSHEET: A DEEPER DIVE INTO YOUR ACS

What did you love as a child?

What activities are fun for you?

What parts of your culture do you enjoy engaging in?

What makes you laugh?

What were you born with that no one can take away?

What do you base your self-worth on?

What would your friends and family value about you?

What are your sources of strength and resilience?

What brought you meaning and purpose today?

Who are you beneath the waves of changing thoughts and emotions?

What brings you joy?

What makes you curious?

What do you feel compassion toward?

What made you feel awe today?

How do you use your intersecting identities to engage the world?

Guided Meditation to Meet Your Authentic Confident Self

Feeling stuck, or unable to visualize a clear version of your ACS? This guided meditation will take you on a powerful inner journey using relaxation and visualization to bring that version of you into clear focus — not just as an idea, but as a presence you can feel, hear, and embody through a guided visualization.

Find a comfortable position where your body is resting and relaxed. Scan your body to make sure all parts are supported and calm.

Take a deep breath, inhaling through your nose while exhaling through your mouth. Continue these deep breaths for five rounds, trying to extend and elongate the inhales and exhales as you go.

Notice any tension held in your body and invite those parts to relax. Notice any thoughts crossing your mind and bring your focus back to your breath.

Inhale white, calming light, and exhale any stress or tension. Inhale confidence, exhale doubt. Inhale peace, exhale negativity.

Now bring to mind your favorite, safest place in nature. Seeing it from a distance, start to step down a stone flight of stairs leading into your serene nature landscape. As you count down the steps, notice your body going even deeper into relaxation. 10, 9, 8, 7, 6, 5, 4, 3, 2...1.

Find a comfortable seat in your favorite nature spot and absorb all the sights and sounds around you. What colors are in your nature scene? What peaceful sounds? What relaxing noises are present?

As you relax into your scene, visualize your most Authentic, Confident, Self, (ACS) walking towards you.
Notice what they are wearing. How do they hold themselves? What energy is emanating from them? What color is their hair? Their clothes? How does their presence make you feel? Take a few moments here to observe your ACS in front of you in your safe place.

Spend time sitting, talking or walking with your Authentic Confident version of self. Ask any questions you feel compelled to ask. Soak up their energy and vibe. Absorb any wisdom that is being sent on to you in this moment.

Whenever you feel your time together has ended, hug your ACS and feel their positive energy transmitting to every cell in your body.

Slowly walk back up the steps into the present, moving your fingers and toes, bringing awareness back into your body.

Feel free to journal what wisdom you learned, or ways that you can emulate this version of self in your day-to-day.

CHAPTER 3 CHEAT SHEET: AUTHENTIC CONFIDENT SELF

- Rediscover joy and inspiration. Reflect on what activities made you feel joyful and inspired as a child. These moments help reconnect you with your authentic self.
- Identify your core strengths. Take time to recognize your unique strengths—qualities that come naturally and make you feel capable and confident.
- Clarify your core values. Define the principles that guide your life and give it meaning. Living in alignment with your values strengthens your sense of authenticity.
- Practice confidence rituals. Build habits and rituals of boosting your ACS as a part of your daily routine.
- Create a Personal Confidence Blueprint. Combine your core strengths, values, and confidence rituals into a guide that keeps you grounded in who you are.
- Practice confidence daily. Confidence is like a muscle—it grows through small, consistent actions such as speaking up, setting boundaries, or trying something new.
- Protect your confidence. Set boundaries against negative influences and avoid the comparison trap by focusing on your own progress and achievements.
- Celebrate your progress! Regularly reflect on and celebrate your wins, no matter how small, to reinforce your sense of self-worth.

Chapter 4: Coping with the Emotional & Cognitive Storms

Emotions are like waves — they rise, crest, and eventually recede. But for many of us, those waves can sometimes feel overwhelming and even relentless. No matter our personal history or current circumstances, we all can recall times of emotional turbulence—moments when feelings like sadness, worry, anger, or self-doubt surged with intensity.

While our instinct may be to avoid or escape these uncomfortable emotions at any cost, they often carry important messages for our human journey. In moderation, these emotions serve a purpose — lessons to be learned, wisdom to be gained, or depths of the human experience to be reached. And with the right tools, they don't have to totally consume us.

Learning how to regulate and respond to uncomfortable emotions — rather than be swept away by them — is a key step toward cultivating calm, resilience, and lasting emotional well-being. The four main categories of uncomfortable emotions we will be discussing in the coming chapters correlate with the four main emotion labels from our Feelings List: Sadness, Worry, Self-doubt, and Anger.

SADNESS

Sadness sucks, especially when it seems endless and inescapable. No one wants to live under the cloud of depression day in and day out. But whether our sadness feels mild or deep and intense—the key isn't avoiding it altogether, but to keep it from stacking up unchecked.

Instead of trying to escape it, we can work on addressing our sadness as it shows up, trigger by trigger. Using healthy coping strategies and staying aware, we can slowly chip away at the cloud. And over time, with patience and effort, we rise above it.

Sadness often carries a stigma, as though feeling it is a weakness. But sadness isn't inherently bad. In fact, it's one of the most deeply human emotions we all share—it connects us to ourselves, to others, and to the broader human experience. Without sadness, empathy would be hard to cultivate. It allows us to mourn losses, process pain, and seek comfort and connection.

Sadness becomes problematic, however, when it isn't processed or soothed. Unresolved sadness can grow into something much heavier—depression. When sadness is prolonged and overwhelming, it can trigger the brain's *fight, flight, or freeze* system into a shutdown response in order to protect itself. This state of *hypoactivation* leaves us feeling numb, disconnected, and unable to engage with life.

In short-term therapy, sadness is treated not as an enemy to be defeated but as a signal to be acknowledged and addressed. Together we can learn to sit with the emotion, understand its message, and use healthy coping strategies to move through it.

SADNESS: OLD BELIEFS THAT REV UP THE AMYGDALA

When we're experiencing sadness, there are certain recurring thoughts that tend to amplify the emotion by keeping the amygdala—the brain's emotional alarm system—on high alert. These thoughts, often ingrained from past experiences, create a loop that reinforces sadness. Common examples include:

- "I am alone."
- "Things will never get better."
- "I will never get what I want."
- "I am not enough."
- "I do not belong."
- "I will never get through this pain."
- "I hate myself."
- "There is no hope."
- "Life is too unfair."
- "I am broken."
- "People will not choose me."

One of the most effective ways to regulate sadness, as well as other uncomfortable emotions we will discuss in later chapters, is through Cognitive Behavioral Therapy (CBT) tools. These beliefs, though they may feel real in the moment, can be distortions—stories our minds create when we're overwhelmed by emotions. Cognitive distortions are thought patterns that many of us repeat on autopilot. They are so common in fact, that CBT researchers have created a top ten list of the most reported distortions.

As we go through each emotion and its description that follows, we will untwist these distortions with five cognitive behavioral therapy techniques to decrease our maladaptive thinking patterns that add to each negative emotion. Remember: repetition is key!

Top Ten Cognitive Distortions:

1. **All-or-Nothing Thinking:** Viewing situations in extreme terms, as either all good or all bad, without acknowledging shades of gray.

2. **Overgeneralization:** Seeing a pattern and drawing conclusions based on one single negative event, as if it proves a general truth.

3. **Mental Filtering:** Only paying attention to the negative aspects of a situation while ignoring positive ones.

4. **Discounting the Positive:** Dismissing or undervaluing positive experiences or achievements, often attributing them to luck or external factors.

5. **Jumping to Conclusions:** Imagining what we think others are thinking or predicting the future negatively without sufficient evidence.

6. **Magnification:** Blowing things out of proportion, maximizing the importance of negative events while minimizing the importance of positive ones.

7. **Emotional Reasoning:** Assuming that if we feel a certain way, it must be true and accurately reflect reality, without considering other evidence.

8. **"Should" Statements:** Using critical "should," "ought," or "must" statements to oneself or others, often based on unrealistic expectations.

9. **Labeling:** Assigning labels or broad beliefs to oneself or others based on a single negative event.

10. **Personalization:** Blaming yourself or taking responsibility for events that are outside of your control or caused by external factors.

CBT focuses on identifying and changing the cognitive distortions that fuel emotional distress. Throughout the chapters that will follow, we will first review five thought-questioning CBT tools before diving into the more detailed, hands-on regulation coping skills.

Five CBT tools to transform old beliefs into new beliefs:

1. **Replace Old Beliefs**

    Whenever you catch yourself spiraling into negative thought patterns, pause and consciously replace those thoughts with new, healthier beliefs. Even if the new belief doesn't feel true right away, repeating it helps to create new neural pathways. *Neurons that fire together, wire together.* Over time, the brain learns to default to these healthier patterns.

2. **Test the Evidence**

    Sad thoughts are often based on assumptions rather than facts. A useful CBT technique is to test the evidence by asking yourself:

    - "What evidence do I have that this thought is true?"
    - "What's the most likely outcome?"
    - "Would my loved ones say this is factual?"

    By questioning your thoughts, you engage the PFC and reduce sadness.

3. **Repeat a Self-Compassion Mantra**

   When sadness feels overwhelming, repeating a soothing mantra can help ground you. Choose a phrase that feels comforting, such as:

   - "This too shall pass."
   - "I'm doing the best I can."
   - "I am worthy of love and care."

   Repeat the mantra slowly and gently, either silently or out loud, until you feel a sense of calm returning.

4. **Reframe the Narrative**

   Reframing sad-inducing situations can help shift your mindset. For example, if someone ghosted you after a promising date, instead of staying sad, you could reframe it as, "They weren't right for me, and I just dodged a bullet." Finding purpose or meaning in frustrating events helps reduce emotional intensity.

5. **Help or Harm**

   Notice the specific sad thoughts that come up most often for you. Ask yourself, do these thoughts help you or harm you? Are they getting you closer to your goals of self-confidence, or are they triggering your amygdala and making you more

   stressed out? Try to be the guard dog at the gate of your brain, only allowing in helpful thoughts and letting go of harmful ones.

SELF-REFLECTION WORKSHEET

What negative beliefs do you notice that add to your sad stress responses?

Which type of cognitive distortion are these beliefs?

SADNESS: NEW BELIEFS THAT REV UP THE PFC

The goal is to shift from these old, automatic thoughts to new, empowering beliefs that activate the prefrontal cortex (PFC), the part of the brain responsible for logic, empathy, and emotional regulation. By doing so, we create space for hope, resilience, and perspective.

Now that we've conquered the practice of mindfulness and built up our ACS, we can much more easily observe which thought patterns are distortions. Once we acknowledge our sad cognitions, we can change them.

Putting our old cognitive distortions through the five filters above can lead to healthier beliefs we can put into practice when sadness arises.

SOME HEALTHIER BELIEFS WE MIGHT ADOPT INCLUDE:

- "This is a temporary emotional experience, not a permanent state."
- "I can find moments of hope, even in difficult times."
- "I am not alone; there are people who care about me."
- "I can focus on what I have, rather than what I lack."
- "Everyone experiences sadness—it's part of being human."
- "I have survived hard times before, and I can do it again."
- "I am worthy of love, just as I am."

- "Grief is a natural part of life. I can learn to live with it."
- "I can create meaning from this pain."
- "Nothing is permanent—this feeling will pass."
- "There are people and experiences that bring joy into my life."
- "I can reach out for support when I need it."
- "This is just a temporary emotional sensation, it doesn't have to be a universal truth."
- "I can be grateful for what I DO have in my life today, even though I am sad I don't have all the goals reached yet."
- "I can create ANY story that makes me feel better about this situation."
- "My birthright, like every other human, is to be loved and give love. I am worthy of love. I am no different."
- "You can go back in time and be the parent you needed in times of valid sadness and pain."
- "By not giving up, holding the vision, and by keeping my standards high I will find what I want both internally and externally."
- "I deserve and am worthy of the love I want and need."

- "There are inspiring people out there who have persevered and found exactly what I am looking for."

- "Loss, grief, and disappointment are a reality of every human's life, and I am practicing how to relate and befriend that truth, where others may be dodging it."

- "I can practice healthy ways to cope with pain."

- "Nothing is permanent, everything changes. My sadness will pass."

- "I see many kind, loving friends and supports that have been reflected on my journey."

- "I am not alone in feeling this way and can reach out for help if I need a connection."

- "We are breathing the air of an oppressive patriarchal system. The effects of racial, sexual, or gender discrimination is real and impactful. I am not alone."

SELF-REFLECTION WORKSHEET

What beliefs do you notice that soothe your sad stress responses?

Which tools did you use to change the cognitive distortions?

These new beliefs don't erase sadness—they offer a way to work with it, to hold space for it without letting it take over completely. The more we practice these beliefs, the more we strengthen the neural pathways associated with calm and confidence.

COPING SKILLS TO REGULATE SADNESS

While changing thought patterns is a powerful long-term strategy, navigating sadness in the *moment* often requires additional tools. When emotions feel overwhelming, it helps to have practical techniques you can turn to right away.

Below are several **evidence-based coping skills** to support you through the emotional storm of sadness:

1. **Schedule a Crying Break**
   Crying is a natural and effective way to release sadness. Instead of suppressing the urge to cry, give yourself permission to do it intentionally. Set a timer for 15 minutes and allow yourself to cry without judgment. When the timer goes off, take a deep breath, thank yourself for processing your emotions, and gently transition to another activity.

2. **Soothe Your Sadness Like You Would a Child**
   Think of your sadness as an inner child needing comfort and reassurance. If a three-year-old came to you in tears because they had lost their favorite toy, you wouldn't respond with criticism or impatience. You'd likely speak with kindness, offering understanding and soothing words. The same approach can be applied to your own sadness.
   Try talking to yourself with gentle compassion, as though you're nurturing that inner child who feels hurt. Phrases like "It's okay to feel this way" or "I'm here for you" can help create a sense of safety and

care within yourself. Most times our inner child and sad parts are seeking some form of connection. Reach out to a trusted friend, join a supportive community, or even engage in virtual spaces where you feel seen and heard. Human connection reminds us that we are not alone in our struggles.

3. **Pendulate Between Sadness and Safety**

Pendulation is a technique used in trauma therapy where you move your attention between a distressing sensation and a neutral or pleasant one. If you feel sadness in your chest, for example, you might pendulate between that feeling and the sensation of your feet on the ground. This helps create balance and prevents emotional overwhelm.

4. **Tune Into Your Body**

Peter Levine's work on somatic experiencing emphasizes the importance of listening to the body's signals. When you feel sadness, take a moment to locate it in your body. Is it in your chest, throat, or stomach? What does it feel like—tight, heavy, or warm? Visualize a white light entering your body through your toes, relaxing and soothing every cell in your body. Bring your focus to how the white light arrives at each part of your body. Starting from your toes and working up to your head, notice where you feel your sadness. This practice reduces physical tension caused by sadness and helps calm the mind. By observing and naming these sensations, you shift focus away from overwhelming thoughts and into the present moment, which can help regulate the nervous system.

5. **Try The Rain Method**

The RAIN method, popularized by psychologist and mindfulness teacher Tara Brach, is a powerful way to process difficult emotions like sadness. The acronym stands for: Recognize the emotion (acknowledge that sadness is present). Accept it (allow the emotion to be there without resistance).

Investigate it (explore what thoughts or sensations accompany the sadness). Nurture yourself (offer self-compassion and care). Take a moment to close your eyes, breathe deeply, and ask your sadness, "What do you need right now?" You may be surprised by the answer. It might be something simple like rest, comfort, connection, or creative expression.

This practice helps you create space for your emotions without becoming overwhelmed by them.

6. **Wrap It in a Blanket Visualization**

   When sadness feels too overwhelming and it's not the right time to fully engage with it, you can use visualization to contain it temporarily. Imagine gently wrapping your sadness in a soft, warm blanket and tucking it into a safe, quiet corner of your mind. This doesn't mean ignoring your feelings—it's about giving them a place to rest until you're ready to address them fully.

7. **Express Yourself Creatively**

   Sadness can be transformed into something beautiful through creative expression. Whether it's writing, painting, composing music, or crafting, giving voice to your feelings in a creative way can help release and process them. Remember, some of the greatest art and music in history were born from moments of profound sadness.

8. **Find Positive Meaning**

   Even in difficult situations, it's possible to find meaning or a silver lining. This doesn't mean denying the pain—it's about balancing the narrative by acknowledging that something valuable may come from the experience. For instance,

whenever I feel overwhelming sadness, I remember that as I work through it, I am gaining valuable insights that I can teach others. Without my sad moments, I could not connect deeply with others' sad moments.

9. **Do Research for Perspective**

Sometimes learning about how others have navigated sadness can help normalize your experience. Whether it's reading memoirs, listening to podcasts, or watching documentaries, seeing how others have coped with similar emotions can provide inspiration and hope.

10. **Rewrite the Story**

We often create stories around our experiences that amplify sadness. For example, after a disappointment, you might tell

yourself, "This always happens to me" or "I'll never succeed." Try rewriting the narrative with a more empowering perspective. Instead of focusing on what you don't have, emphasize what you've learned or how you've grown. As Brené Brown suggests in her book *Rising Strong*, choosing how to frame your story can shift your emotional experience.

11. **Progressive Muscle Relaxation**

Progressive muscle relaxation (PMR) is a well-known technique for calming both the body and mind. It involves tensing and then slowly relaxing each muscle group, starting from your toes and working up to your head. As you release tension, you'll notice a corresponding sense of calm and ease in your emotions. Guided PMR exercises can be found online if you're new to the practice.

12. Notice "Glimmers"

In psychology, a "glimmer" is the opposite of a trigger. It's a brief, positive experience that activates the parasympathetic nervous system—the part of your nervous system responsible for rest, calm, and relaxation. While triggers activate stress and sadness, glimmers can create moments of comfort and joy. The key is to intentionally notice and savor these small, positive experiences throughout your day.

Examples of glimmers might include:

The warmth of sunlight on your skin.

The sound of a loved one's laughter.

A random act of kindness from a stranger.

By training your brain to notice glimmers, you gradually increase your capacity for positive emotions and reduce the intensity of sadness. When sadness makes everything feel heavy, shifting your attention to the small, everyday miracles around you can be a powerful mood booster. Whether it's the beauty of a sunset, the intricate pattern of frost on a window, or the joy of a pet's companionship, focusing on these moments of wonder can remind you that life holds beauty even in difficult times.

13. Build gratitude

Gratitude isn't about forcing yourself to feel thankful when life feels tough. Instead, it's about noticing what's already there—focusing in on what you DO have instead of what you don't have. Being triggered, sad, and stressed cannot exist in our bodies at the exact same time as holding appreciation and gratitude.

For a quick boost, place your hand on your chest and intentionally focus on three things you are grateful for. The more emotionally salient, the better. Become creative with your gratitude list instead of repeating the same things over every day. Intentionally list what you appreciate both about yourself internally, and what is surrounding you externally. Millions of humans around the world are currently starving, and exposed to war, trauma, and death daily. Soothe sadness by remembering appreciation.

14. **Lean Into Your Protective Factors**

    When sadness feels overwhelming, it's helpful to focus on your protective factors—the people, values, and resources that support your mental well-being. These might include:

    Strong relationships with family or friends.

    Spiritual or religious beliefs that offer comfort and hope.

    Personal goals or dreams that give you a sense of purpose.

    Hobbies and activities that bring you joy.

    By leaning into these protective factors, you remind yourself of the parts of life that provide stability and meaning, even in the face of sadness.

15. **Engage Your Senses**

    One of the quickest ways to shift out of an emotional storm is to engage your five senses. This technique, often used in Dialectical Behavior Therapy (DBT), helps bring your attention back to the present moment by focusing on sensory experiences:

    - Sight: Look around and find five things that catch your eye.

- Sound: Listen closely to the sounds around you, both near and far.
- Touch: Notice how your clothes feel against your skin or the texture of an object in your hand.
- Smell: Take a deep breath and notice any scents in your environment.
- Taste: Slowly savor a piece of food or a drink, focusing on its flavor.

This grounding technique helps regulate your emotions by redirecting attention from distressing thoughts to your immediate experience.

EXPLORE SUBCONSCIOUS PAST WOUNDS WITH ANY EMOTIONS:

Sometimes sadness isn't just about what's happening in the present—it can be rooted in unresolved emotional wounds from the past.

For example, childhood experiences of rejection or neglect may leave lingering feelings of sadness that resurface in adulthood.
When you notice recurring patterns of sadness, it can be helpful to explore these deeper layers with curiosity and compassion.

One effective technique is to write a letter to your younger self, offering the reassurance, love, and support you needed back then. This practice helps heal old wounds by giving your inner child a voice and acknowledging the validity of their feelings. Over time, this can reduce the intensity of sadness tied to past experiences.

However, if you're still noticing moments of sadness that the previous coping skills don't help with, a guided meditation can be an added coping skill option. A guided meditation can be done when you have time to put aside for deeper relaxation and intentionality around exploring your sadness.

Similarly to the ACS guided visualization, this tool helps you access deeper parts of the brain and psyche.

This guided meditation is designed to be flexible, and you can interchange any uncomfortable or lingering emotion you are hoping to ease.

Guided Meditation to Heal Core Sadness Wounds

Find a comfortable position where your body is resting and relaxed. Scan your body to make sure all parts are supported and calm.

Take a deep breath, inhaling through your nose and exhaling through your mouth. Continue for five rounds, trying to extend and elongate the inhales and exhales.

Notice any tension held in your body and invite those parts to relax. Notice any thoughts that come to mind, and bring your focus back to your breath.

Inhale white, calming light, and exhale any stress or tension. Inhale confidence, exhale doubt. Inhale peace, exhale negativity.

Now bring to mind your safest, most peaceful place in nature. Seeing it from a distance, start to descend a stone flight of stairs leading into your serene natural landscape. As you count down the steps, notice your body going even deeper into relaxation. 10, 9, 8, 7, 6, 5, 4, 3, 2...1.

Find a comfortable seat in your favorite nature spot and absorb all the sights and sounds around you. Notice the colors, peaceful sounds, and relaxing noises.

As you relax into your scene, visualize your most Authentic, Confident, Self, (ACS) walking towards you. As you sit together, bring to mind the sadness you have been carrying. With the support of your authentic self, ask the sadness how old it is. How long has it been present in your body? When was it first created? Why was it first created?

Visualize yourself going back in time to the moment when your sadness first began. How old were you? Who is involved? What situation is causing this sad part of you? Who is triggering this sadness?

Ask your authentic self to step forward and give yourself anything you need in this scene to rewrite the narrative and protect yourself from this emotional imprint of sadness. What do you need to feel safe, feel heard, seen, and taken care of? Stay in this scene absorbing as much support as needed from your healed, authentic self.

Notice what maladaptive beliefs you created as a child in this scene related to your sadness. Take as much time as you need to offer your younger self wisdom, care, and new, truthful, adaptive belief systems.

Whenever you feel your time together has come to a close, hug your authentic, confident self and feel their positive energy transmitting to every cell in your body. Slowly walk back up the steps into the present, moving your fingers and toes to bring awareness back into your body.

Feel free to journal what wisdom you learned and how this early childhood scene impacts your emotional landscape today.

15 COPING SKILLS FOR SADNESS

1. Crying Break
2. Soothe and Seek Connection
3. Pendulate From Sad to Safety
4. Tuning into Your Body
5. RAIN
6. Blanket visualization
7. Create Art
8. Find Any Positive Meaning
9. Research
10. Rewrite the story
11. Progressive Muscle Relaxation
12. Find Glimmers & Miracles
13. Practice Gratitude
14. Lean into Protective Factors
15. Grounding Through the Five Senses

YOUR COPING SKILLS TO MANAGE SADNESS

1. _____
2. _____
3. _____
4. _____
5. _____
6. _____
7. _____
8. _____
9. _____
10. _____

CHAPTER 4 CHEAT SHEET: BRAIN WORKOUT PLAN TO COPE WITH SADNESS

Just like building our physical bodies, repetition in our mental coping habits can lead to growth and strength. Below are three steps to follow as a routine for strengthening your emotional resilience:

- **Step into your mindful awareness.** Whenever sadness arises, pause and notice what your emotional mind is thinking and feeling.
- **Activate your authentic self.** From a place of compassion, choose one or more coping skills that your authentic self can offer your sad part. Choose whatever resonates with you in the moment.
- **Practice consistently.** The key to rewiring your brain is repetition. Each time you practice a coping skill, you're reinforcing healthier neural pathways that help you manage sadness more effectively.

WORRY

Social anxiety is one of the top reasons students seek help at college counseling centers—over 70% report it as their main concern. This isn't surprising. Our nervous systems have been wired for constant alertness, shaped by a society that often rewards hustle, comparison, and perfectionism.

At some point, *everyone* has experienced that familiar anxious loop—the racing thoughts, the sleepless nights, and the endless "what if" spirals.

And while the anxious part of us believes it's being helpful—protecting us, pushing us toward success—in reality, it often does the opposite. It drains our energy, clouds our focus, and convinces us that we're not enough.

The good news? That anxious part can be *soothed*. It can be spoken to, calmed and asked to rest. With the right coping skills, we don't have to fight anxiety—we can learn to listen to it, respond with compassion, and slowly take back control.

Worry and fear often get a bad reputation, but they play an essential role in helping us navigate life's uncertainties. Without worry, we wouldn't plan ahead or prepare for potential risks. Without fear, we wouldn't know when to protect ourselves from danger. However, when worry and fear become chronic or excessive, they can take a toll on our mental health, leading to anxiety and stress.

Fear is an instinctive response to immediate danger, while worry is the mind's attempt to anticipate and solve future problems.

Both are designed to keep us safe, but when they become overactive, they can trap us in cycles of overthinking and avoidance.

In a short-term therapy approach, we can learn to manage worry and fear by regulating our thoughts and using targeted coping strategies to calm the nervous system.

WORRY: OLD BELIEFS THAT REV UP THE AMYGDALA

Much like with sadness, habitual thought patterns tend to rev up the amygdala, heightening our sense of fear and worry. These thoughts create a feedback loop where anxious thoughts fuel emotional distress, and emotional distress, in turn, reinforces anxious thoughts.

Common examples include:

- "It will not work out."
- "I will fail."
- "Something bad is going to happen."
- "People will judge me."
- "I won't be able to handle this discomfort."
- "The worst-case scenario is inevitable."
- "I am not strong enough to deal with this."
- "I will never feel safe."
- "This pain will get worse and never end."
- "I have no control over what happens."

These thoughts, though automatic, are rarely accurate reflections of reality. They're distortions—exaggerated stories we tell ourselves in moments of fear.

SELF-REFLECTION WORKSHEET

What negative beliefs do you notice that add to your worry stress responses?

Which type of cognitive distortion are these beliefs?

WORRY: NEW BELIEFS THAT REV UP THE PFC

To regulate worry, we can shift from these old, fear-based beliefs to new, empowering thoughts that activate the prefrontal cortex (PFC)—just like we did with our sad thought patterns.

High reps equate to faster growth, so use these five CBT tools to transform our worry thought patterns on repeat:

Remember our first step--once we've identified the belief underlying our worry, we want to pass it through our Five CBT tools to rehearse a healthier belief.

Five CBT tools to transform old beliefs into new beliefs:

1. Replace Old Beliefs
2. Test the Evidence
3. Repeat a Self-Compassion Mantra
4. Reframe the Worry Narrative
5. Help or Harm

SOME HEALTHIER BELIEFS WE MIGHT ADOPT INCLUDE:

- "I don't need to solve everything right now."
- "What people think of me does not define my worth."
- "I can only control what's in my power and let go of the rest."
- "I have survived difficult moments before—I can do it again."

- "Even if things don't go perfectly, I can handle the outcome."
- "It's okay to feel uncomfortable; this feeling will pass."
- "By focusing on what I can do today, I will build a better future."
- "I can take small steps toward what I fear, and I will grow stronger."
- "Everyone feels anxious sometimes—I am not alone in this."
- "I will not miss out on what is meant for me."
- "The worst-case scenario is unlikely, and even if it happens, I can cope."
- "I am still worthy of love and belonging, no matter what."
- "Even if I imagine every single terrible scenario, it won't prevent whatever will happen from happening."
- "We will all be gone in 200 years and no one will remember my awkward social interaction."
- "By preparing and giving my best, I will create a good outcome."
- "What people think of me does not define my worth."
- "My identity and worth are not dependent on any external factors. I control the narratives of worth and authenticity of myself, not others."
- "The right people will stay. I'm not going to miss anything meant for me."

- "It's more important to stay true to my authentic self than trying to get approval by being fake."
- "I will be okay if I disappoint people."
- "All emotions pass."
- "I can let go and accept what I cannot control."
- "I am still loved and worthy even when I fail, lose, or make a mistake."
- "If I don't give up and work hard, my dreams will come true."
- "Failure and conflict are the best way to learn and grow."
- "I can take small steps towards doing what I am anxious about."
- "My future self is proud of me on the other side for enduring this uncomfortable feeling."
- "Everyone here is thinking about their own worries, not judging me."
- "A year from now, no one will remember this."

SELF-REFLECTION WORKSHEET

What healthy beliefs do you notice that soothe your worry/stress responses?

Which tools did you use to change the cognitive distortions?

COPING SKILLS TO REGULATE YOUR WORRY

Below is a comprehensive list of tools and strategies to help manage worry and fear. These methods activate the PFC, calm the amygdala, and promote emotional regulation. Using mindfulness, notice where you feel the emotion in your body. Notice which thoughts are fueling this emotion. Then choose from some of the evidence-based coping skills below.

1. **Talk to yourself like you would talk to your BFF**

   We can be our own harshest critics! Sometimes the fears we tell ourselves are things we would never say to a beloved best friend. Anytime you notice racing, negative anxious thought patterns ask yourself, "What would I say to my best friend who is having these same thoughts?" Most times that response is a lot kinder and warmer than what we say internally to ourselves. Repeat your best friend's advice over and over inside your own mind to decrease worry thoughts.

2. **Schedule a Worry Break**

   Instead of letting worry dominate your entire day, set aside a specific time to think about your concerns—perhaps 30 minutes in the evening. When the time is up, gently remind yourself that you've given worry its space and it's now time to move on.

3. **Go for a Walk**

   Physical movement helps release built-up stress hormones and increases the production of endorphins, the body's natural feel-good chemicals. Walking outdoors, especially in nature, can enhance this effect by engaging our senses. When our eyes are scanning the landscape in front of us, our nervous system is told that we are safe and no threats are present.

4. Try Safe Space Visualization

Imagine a place where you feel completely safe—maybe a cozy room, a peaceful forest, or a beach. Close your eyes, breathe deeply, and picture yourself in this safe space. This visualization helps calm your nervous system and provides a mental retreat from worry. When we imagine a safe, calming space, our brains believe we are IN that safe calming space. If we practice this skill daily our brain pathways will get more and more practice tapping into the feel-good chemicals of our safe space.

For example, whenever I feel overwhelmed or worried, I imagine I am underwater in the river near my childhood home. I see clear, endless blue-green water, broken by bright white beams of sunlight. I feel it on my hot skin, cool and refreshing. I hear complete peace and quiet. When we put effort into visualizing all five senses in our safe place, good chemicals are released, and less *fight, flight, or freeze* activation will be triggered.

Come up with your own safe space visualization to pull out of your pocket at any time when anxiety arises.

5. Use your Breath

When you breathe deeply with an extended exhale, it signals to your brain that you are safe. Deep breathing activates the nervous system, which controls how the body rests. This can cause your heart rate to slow and your blood pressure to drop. Inhaling for four counts and exhaling for eight counts can quickly reduce anxiety, alerting your nervous system that there is no hypothetical lion in the room.

Box-breathing can also be a helpful visualization tool. Mentally picture your favorite shape and trace the outline of it by alternating deep inhales and exhales on each side. For example, trace up one line of a square with a deep inhale, and trace the adjacent side with a deep exhale. Counting to 4 on each breath helps keep focus signaling to the rest of the body that there is no danger present.

6. **Sigh/Humming**

Research shows that sighing—a long exhale following a quick inhale—helps reset the nervous system and calm worry. Take a quick double inhale through your nose, then exhale fully through your mouth in a long sigh. Repeat 3-5 times to reduce tension. Big sighs also can give your lungs an air boost and improve your blood pressure. Singing or humming helps stimulate the vagus nerve, which plays a crucial role in calming the nervous system. Even a few minutes of humming your favorite tune can reduce the physical symptoms of anxiety.

Singing and humming actually strengthens our vagal tone, sending new signals of calm and relaxation from the brain stem throughout our whole body. Likewise, it also helps regulate a healthy heart rate variability. Singing also helps release the pent-up stress chemicals stored with emotions.

7. **Face Your Fears Gradually**

Avoiding situations that trigger worry may provide short-term relief, but it often reinforces anxiety in the long run. Gradual exposure—facing fears one step at a time—helps reduce the intensity of worry over time. Create a step by step list of triggering events, and visualize a calming, soothing place or mantra alongside each step. Conquer one before moving on to the next. Over time you will trick your brain like Pavlov's dog to a conditioned calm around all aspects of your fear.

How to practice:

- Make a list of situations that trigger your anxiety, ranked from least to most distressing.
- Start with the least distressing situation and expose yourself to it in a controlled, safe way.
- Use calming techniques like deep breathing while facing the situation.
- Gradually work your way up the list.

8. Make a Plan to Prepare

Worry often stems from uncertainty. Creating a plan to solve a problem can provide a sense of control and reduce anxiety.

How to practice:

- Identify the situation causing worry.
- Break it down into smaller, manageable steps.
- Find solutions to help address the issues at hand.
- Create a timeline or to-do list for each step.
- Take action one step at a time.

Giving a presentation? Memorize those slides so you know you will crush it! Anxious about a blind date? Prepare a set of questions and conversation starters that will make you feel in control and confident.

9. Ask "So What?"

When worry leads to catastrophic thinking, asking, "So what if that happens?" can help reduce the intensity of anxious thoughts.

Example:

- Worry: "What if I mess up during my presentation?"
- Response: "So what if I mess up? I'll learn from it, and it's not the end of the world."

For myself, my anxiety ramps up when I walk into my boss's office for my yearly performance review. If I get bad feedback, so what? I can grow, learn, and take constructive criticism.

Walking into a party, worried someone will judge your outfit, so what? Their opinion of your fashion doesn't matter at all, as long as you feel your hottest self.

10. Try Tapping (EFT)

Emotional Freedom Technique (EFT), or tapping, involves tapping on specific acupressure points while focusing on a worry-inducing thought. This practice helps reduce the emotional charge of the thought.

How to practice:

- Identify a specific worry.
- Tap gently on these points while repeating a calming phrase.
- The side of your hand.
- Your eyebrows.
- The side of your eyes.
- Under your nose.
- Your chin.
- Your collarbone.
- Continue until you feel calmer.

11. Focus on One Small Thing You Can Control

When worry feels overwhelming, shifting your attention to something you can control—no matter how small—can help ground you.

For example: If you're worried about an upcoming event, focus on preparing what you'll wear or organizing your notes. This gives you a sense of agency in the situation.

12. Engage in a Pleasurable Activity

When you're caught in a loop of worry, shifting your focus to something enjoyable can help disrupt the cycle. Choose an activity that brings you joy—whether it's reading a book, playing a game, or spending time with a pet.

Sometimes our American culture can glorify an over-functioning work ethic. Giving our brains a break from constant problem-solving and hustling can actually increase productivity outcomes. Just like filling up gas in a car, we need feel-good fuel to keep running smoothly. Make a list of activities that bring you pleasure to bust worry. Sports, game nights, movies, shopping, cooking, anything that you enjoy. Google a list of pleasurable activities if you run out of exciting ideas!

13. Organize Your Environment

Clutter and disorganization can contribute to feelings of overwhelm. Taking a few minutes to tidy up your space can reduce mental clutter and promote calm. Organize your to do list in order from most important to least important. Make a daily routine and schedule to increase feelings of control and predictability.

14. Take a sensory break

Sometimes overstimulation of our senses can add to the sense of panic and worry. When you notice escalation in your thoughts and body, create a plan for a sensory break. Have a space that is quiet, calm, and soothing. Choose supports such as noise canceling headphones, eyes masks, or a room with dim light. Create your safe sensory space and leave all of your problems outside of that space. Take tokens of peace that remind you of that space if you are out in the world such as worry stones, sunglasses, or headphones.

15. **Binaural beats**

    Listening to binaural beats delivers different sound frequencies that impact your brainwaves. Binaural beats in the higher alpha frequencies (8 to 13 Hz) can decrease anxiety, promote positivity, and encourage relaxation. Binaural beats in the lower beta frequencies (14 to 30 Hz) are correlated to improved memory, problem-solving, increased concentration, and alertness. A quick internet search can help you explore this coping skill.

Guided Meditation to Heal Core Fear Wounds

Find a comfortable position where your body is resting and relaxed. Scan your body to make sure all parts are supported and calm.

Take a deep breath, inhaling through your nose and exhaling through your mouth. Continue for five rounds, trying to extend and elongate the inhales and exhales.

Notice any tension held in your body and invite those parts to relax. Notice any thoughts that come to mind, and bring your focus back to your breath.

Inhale white, calming light, and exhale any stress or tension. Inhale confidence, exhale doubt. Inhale peace, exhale negativity.

Now picture your safest, most peaceful place in nature. Seeing it from a distance, start to descend a stone flight of stairs leading into your serene natural landscape. As you count down the steps, notice your body going even deeper into relaxation. 10, 9, 8, 7, 6, 5, 4, 3, 2.....1.

Find a comfortable seat in your favorite nature spot and absorb all the sights and sounds around you. Notice the colors, peaceful sounds, and relaxing noises.

As you relax into your scene, visualize your most Authentic Confident, Self, (ACS) walking towards you. As you sit together, bring to mind the worry you have been carrying. With the support of your authentic self, ask the worry how old it is. How long has it been present in your body? When was it first created? Why was it first created?

As you sit together, bring to mind the emotion of fear that you have been carrying. With the support of your authentic self, ask the fear how old it is. How long has it been present in your body? When was it first created? Why was it first created?

Visualize yourself going back in time to the moment when your worry first began. How old were you? Who is involved? What situation is causing this worry part of you? Who is triggering this worry?

Ask your authentic self to step forward and give yourself anything you need in this scene to rewrite the narrative and protect yourself from this emotional imprint of worry. What do you need to feel safe, feel heard, seen, and taken care of? Stay in this scene absorbing as much support as needed from your healed, authentic self.

Notice what maladaptive beliefs you created as a child in this scene related to your worry. Take as much time as you need to offer your younger self wisdom, care, and new, truthful, adaptive belief systems.

Whenever you feel your time together has come to a close, hug your Authentic, Confident Self and feel their positive energy transmitting to every cell in your body. Slowly walk back up the steps into the present, moving your fingers and toes to bring awareness back into your body.

Feel free to journal what wisdom you learned and how this early childhood scene impacts your emotional landscape today.

15 COPING SKILLS FOR WORRY	YOUR COPING SKILLS TO MANAGE WORRY
1. BFF Technique	1. _____
2. Worry Break	2. _____
3. Walk	3. _____
4. Safe Space Visualization	4. _____
5. Breathing Techniques	5. _____
6. Sigh/Humming	6. _____
7. Face Your Fears	7. _____
8. Make a Plan to Prepare	8. _____
9. Ask "So what?"	9. _____
10. EFT	10. _____
11. Do One Small Thing	
12. Distract with Pleasurable Activity	
13. Organize Environment	
14. Sensory Break	
15. Listen to Binaural Beat	

CHAPTER 4 CHEAT SHEET: BRAIN WORKOUT PLAN TO COPE WITH WORRY

- **Step into your mindful awareness.** Whenever worry arises, pause and notice what your emotional mind is thinking and feeling.

- **Activate your Authentic Confident Self.** From a place of compassion, choose one or more coping skills that your authentic self can offer your worry part. Choose whatever resonates with you in the moment.

- **Practice consistently.** The key to rewiring your brain is repetition. Each time you practice a coping skill, you're reinforcing healthier neural pathways that help you manage worry more effectively.

SELF-DOUBT

Capitalism generates billions of dollars by making our insecurities worse.

The more inadequate we feel, the more likely we are to buy products that promise to "fix" us. We all can find ourselves stuck on the hedonic treadmill, constantly chasing self-worth through external validation, but never quite reaching it.

Society's lie—that we're not good enough unless we look, act, or consume a certain way—is just that: a lie. And once we become aware of it, we can begin to dismantle it. The coping skills in this chapter are designed to help you challenge that lie and to reconnect with your worth.

Self-doubt can sometimes overshadow lots of areas of our lives, however it also can allow us to reflect, improve, grow, learn, and question. At its core, self-doubt stems from a lack of confidence or belief in one's abilities, worth, or judgment. Negative experiences—such as failures, criticism, or rejection—can contribute to the development of self-doubt by undermining our ability to see our ACS. Internalized messages from caregivers, peers, or authority figures can further influence self-perceptions and contribute to the development of negative self-beliefs.

In a short-term therapy model of care, we can learn to cope with self-doubt and manage it in healthy ways.

To regulate our doubt, we can also adapt and change our thoughts, just like we did with previous emotions.

SELF-DOUBT: OLD BELIEFS THAT REV UP THE AMYGDALA

Similar to sadness and worry, repetitive negative self-talk patterns can keep the amygdala in a hyperactive state, making self-doubt feel overwhelming and true. Common examples include:

- "I suck."
- "I am stupid."
- "I will always fail."
- "I am disappointing my loved ones."
- "I don't fit in or belong here."
- "I will never be as good as them."
- "I am not smart enough."
- "I am not good enough."
- "I don't deserve to be here."
- "I will never be able to accomplish what I want."
- "I won't be able to solve this problem."
- "I am TOO much, TOO _____."
- "Everyone is doing it better than I am."
- "I never finish what I start."
- "I am not _____ enough."

SELF-REFLECTION WORKSHEET

What negative beliefs do you notice that add to your critical stress responses?

Which type of cognitive distortion are these beliefs?

SELF-DOUBT: NEW BELIEFS THAT REV UP THE PFC

By practicing healthier beliefs, we can activate the prefrontal cortex (PFC), which helps regulate emotions and build confidence. These beliefs encourage a shift from doubt-based thinking to logical, supportive thought patterns.

Five CBT tools to transform old beliefs into new beliefs:

1. Replace Old Beliefs
2. Test the Evidence
3. Repeat a Self-Compassion Mantra
4. Reframe the Doubtful Narrative
5. Help or Harm

SOME HEALTHIER BELIEFS WE MIGHT ADOPT INCLUDE:

- "The self-critic won't get me to my goals any faster than my kinder thoughts and will just amp up my fight-or-flight more."
- "My sense of self-love does not have to be correlated to the opinions of others."
- "If I talk to myself with self-compassion, I will have more access to my front brain to solve this problem."
- "I am flexible and adaptable and can fit into differing communities."

- "I am doing my best and can have empathy for others' struggles."
- "I am grateful for what I can bring to the table." I can welcome all emotions, not just the positive ones."
- "My future self will be much better off, and deal with much less pain and despair, if I stay true to my gut and intuition, instead of listening to my inner self-critic."
- "Everyone's timeline on the planet is different for when success happens, and it has no reflection on who I am in all facets of my identity."
- "I am dodging bullets from those who leave because I am going to only choose the ones who choose me."
- "I would much rather be an authentic version of myself than expending energy on masking or being filtered."
- "I have worked very hard to become the best, healed, authentic version of myself, and I am so proud of that journey and the wisdom of my ancestors."
- "Progress, not perfection."
- "My emotions are always valid. My prefrontal cortex is so large. It regulates, processes, and has incredible self-awareness and tools."
- "I am doing the best I can."

- "I am not broken. There are parts of this world that can be traumatic, toxic, and damaging to us all."
- "A million people have done this before. I can do it too."
- "A person out there will love me and be attracted to me no matter my shape, size, or personality."
- "There are 7 billion people on this planet. Stop wasting time trying to convince anyone of your worth."
- "I have a gift and I can use it."
- "Everyone has endless opinions—I know myself best and trust my own intuition."
- "I am just overwhelmed and can give myself a break to rest and regulate.

SELF-REFLECTION WORKSHEET

What healthy beliefs do you notice that soothe your critical stress responses?

Which tools did you use to change the cognitive distortion?

COPING SKILLS TO REGULATE SELF-DOUBT

The following coping strategies can help you manage self-doubt when it arises. By practicing them regularly, you strengthen the PFC and reduce the activation of the amygdala, making it easier to respond to self-doubt with confidence and calm. Using mindfulness, notice where you feel the emotion in your body. Notice which thoughts are fueling this emotion.

1. **Flip the Story**

    Whenever you catch yourself telling a negative story about your abilities, practice flipping it to a more balanced perspective. For example, if your inner critic says, "I always mess things up," you can flip it to, "I've faced challenges before and learned from them." This exercise helps create more balanced narratives over time.

2. **Remember Toxic Cultural Beliefs**

    Recognize that many of your self-doubts may be influenced by societal or cultural narratives. For example, in some cultures, being called "fat" is seen as a compliment, while in others it's considered negative. Implicit and explicit bias exist in all cultures, creating a norm of hierarchy that can be toxic

    and exclusive. Understanding these schemas can help you separate societal expectations from your own personal worth.

3. **Accept**

    Sometimes we don't need to attach or give too much importance to the doubtful feelings we have. Just notice them and accept their presence without judgment. Let them pass by like leaves floating down a stream. By not engaging with them, you allow your brain to focus on healthier thoughts. Accept your imperfections and unique differences.

4. Fake It 'till You Make It

As we've mentioned in earlier chapters, our brains don't always know the difference between imagination and reality in a chemical sense. Taking on a persona of confidence through watching someone you look up to can be a quick confidence hack.

To address my own self-doubt, each night before going out on the town, I used to ask myself "How would Jessica Biel act in this situation?" I would only act and think like I believed Jessica Biel would. Over time those imagined thoughts became my own, growing the confidence muscle. Anyone who reminds you of your authentic self or who you want to be like? Pretend to be in their confident mind until it becomes your own.

5. Call Forward Your ACS in Social Situations

If you find yourself in a social situation where self-doubt is taking over, take a deep breath and mentally call forward your most Authentic Confident Self. This version of you has practiced self-compassion and knows your strengths. Let that part of you take charge of the situation. Be curious, confident, and in a state of connection with whoever is across from you.

6. Repeat Self-Acceptance in Thoughts and Actions

The more you repeat positive beliefs and actions, the more they become part of your neural pathways. Whether it's a mantra, an affirmation, or a daily practice, consistency is what creates lasting change. Self-loving beliefs may take a while to come up with, start with self-accepting thoughts and place them in places where you will see them daily. Save these on your phone wallpaper, your fridge, your mirror. Want to get more confident at something? Repeat the action over and over until you feel more comfortable and on the path to mastery.

7. **Rest**

Sometimes self-doubt arises because our nervous system is in overdrive, leading to a shutdown or freeze response. This can cause procrastination and avoidance. In these moments, instead of pushing through, allow yourself to rest. Once you've recovered, your prefrontal cortex will re-engage, helping you return to tasks with clarity.

8. **Lean Into Spiritual Resources**

If spirituality or faith plays a role in your life, it can be a powerful tool for managing self-doubt. Prayer, meditation, or connecting with a higher power can provide comfort and reassurance when self-doubt feels overwhelming.

Search for truths that align with your spiritual beliefs in books, communities, shows or podcasts. When struggling with body confidence, I found comfort in reading spiritual books that brought focus to the after-life, highlighting that we are not our bodies, but are souls within them.

9. **Listen to Fired-Up Music**

Music has a unique ability to influence mood and energy. Create a playlist of songs that fire you up and increase your confidence. Genres like hip-hop or rap often have empowering lyrics that can shift your mindset before a challenging event. Sometimes allowing yourself to fully experience emotions through music can be healing and energizing.

10. Become Great at Something

Building confidence in one area of your life can help reduce doubt in others. Find something you enjoy and work on becoming great at it. Whether it's a hobby, a professional skill, or a creative outlet, mastery builds confidence and provides a sense of accomplishment.

Find what lights you up. Then do that thing you are good at over and over. Make space for it in your life. Join a group of others who love to do it. Don't compare yourself to others who have been working for decades behind the scenes.

11. Picture Your Successful Self

Visualization is a powerful tool for confidence. Before facing a situation that triggers self-doubt, take a few moments to picture yourself succeeding. Imagine how it feels to achieve your goal—what you're wearing, what you're saying, how others are reacting. This mental rehearsal helps train your brain for success.

One of my favorite confidence-building antidotes is from the great motivational speaker, Tony Robbins, in a recent Tim Ferris podcast. In the early 90s Tony was working with the famous tennis player, Andre Agassi, helping him build confidence after a wrist injury. Instead of focusing on the injury and all the ways the injury could negatively impact his confidence and outcomes, Tony led Andre to visualize over and over again what it would look and feel like to hit the perfect serve. Even if we are not professional athletes, we can use this tool by intentionally picturing what it would look and feel like to be our most successful confident self.

12. Organize Each Hour of Your Day

Self-doubt can feel overwhelming when you're juggling too many responsibilities. Procrastination, decision paralysis, and shut down can take over quickly. Break your day into manageable chunks and create a simple, realistic plan. Build in times for rest, breaks, and rewards. Knowing what you need to do and when can reduce doubt and increase productivity.

13. Focus on One Small Thing

When self-doubt feels all-consuming, shift your focus to one small thing you appreciate about yourself. It could be a personal strength, a past achievement, or something as simple as a physical feature you like. This practice helps balance out negative thoughts by redirecting attention to something positive.

14. Volunteer/Help Others

Sometimes getting outside of our own life experience can expand our perceptions. Focusing on others who are suffering or struggling can offer us a new perspective on what we have to be grateful for. It is easy to get stuck in the comparison game in our age of social media. Volunteering at homeless shelters, local churches or places that represent a cause near and dear to our hearts can boost self-worth as well as showing us our privileges and strengths.

15. Research Your Attachment Style

Our attachment style—formed in childhood—can influence how we experience insecurity, particularly in relationships. Understanding our attachment style can help us decrease self-doubt when interacting with peers and romantic partners. Check out the new book "Secure Love" by Julie Menanno or follow her Instagram account @thesecurerelationship to get quick tips on how to move from insecure feelings to confidence. We will dive into this more in Chapter 7.

Guided Meditation to Heal Core Self-Critical Wounds

Find a comfortable position where your body is resting and relaxed. Scan your body to make sure all parts are supported and calm.

Take a deep breath, inhaling through your nose and exhaling through your mouth. Continue for five rounds, trying to extend and elongate the inhales and exhales as you go.

Notice any tension held in your body and invite those parts to relax. Notice any thoughts crossing your mind and bring your focus back to your breath.

Inhale white, calming light, and exhale any stress or tension. Inhale confidence, exhale doubt. Inhale peace, exhale negativity.

Now picture your safest, most peaceful place in nature. Seeing it from a distance, start to step down a stone flight of stairs leading into your serene nature landscape. As you count down the steps, notice your body going even deeper into relaxation. 10, 9, 8, 7, 6, 5, 4, 3, 2.....1.

Find a comfortable seat in your favorite nature spot and absorb all the sights and sounds around you. What colors are in your nature scene? What peaceful sounds? Relaxing noises?

As you relax into your scene, visualize your most Authentic, Confident, Self, (ACS) walking towards you.

As you sit together, bring to mind the emotion of self-doubt that you have been carrying. With the support of your authentic self, ask the self-doubt how old it is. How long has it been present in your body? When was it first created? Why was it first created?

Visualize yourself going back in time to the scene where your self-doubt was first created. How old were you? Who is involved? What situation is occurring that created this self-doubt part in you? Who is triggering this self-doubt?

Ask your authentic self to step forward and give you anything you need in this scene to rewrite the narrative and protect yourself from this emotional imprint of self-doubt. What do you need to feel safe? What do you need to feel heard, seen, and taken care of? Stay in this scene absorbing as much support as needed from your healed, authentic self.

Notice what maladaptive beliefs you created as a child in this scene related to your self-doubt. Take as much time as you need to offer your younger self wisdom, care, and new, truthful, adaptive belief systems.

Whenever you feel your time together has come to a close, hug your authentic, confident self and feel their positive energy transmitting to every cell in your body. Slowly walk back up the steps into the present, moving your fingers and toes, bringing awareness back into your body in the present.

Feel free to journal what wisdom you learned and how this early childhood scene impacts your emotional landscape today.

15 COPING SKILLS FOR SELF-DOUBT	**YOUR COPING SKILLS TO MANAGE SELF-DOUBT**
1. Flip the Story	1. _____
2. Remember Toxic Cultural Beliefs	2. _____
3. Accept	3. _____
4. Fake it 'till you make it	4. _____
5. Call Forth ACS	
6. Repeat Self-Acceptance	5. _____
7. Rest	6. _____
8. Lean Into Spirituality	7. _____
9. Make a Playlist	
10. Become Great at Something	8. _____
11. Picture Success	9. _____
12. Organize Your Day	10. _____
13. Focus on One Small Thing	
14. Volunteer/Help Others	
15. Learn Your Attachment Style	

CHAPTER 4 CHEAT SHEET: BRAIN WORKOUT PLAN TO COPE WITH SELF-DOUBT

- **Step into your mindful awareness.** Whenever self-doubt arises, pause and notice what your emotional mind is thinking and feeling.

- **Activate your authentic self.** From a place of compassion, choose one or more coping skills that your authentic self can offer your self-doubt part. Choose whatever resonates with you in the moment.

- **Practice consistently.** The key to rewiring your brain is repetition. Each time you practice a coping skill, you're reinforcing healthier neural pathways that help you manage self-doubt more effectively.

ANGER

Anger can be addictive—especially in today's culture. Housewives flipping over tables has become a very popular form of entertainment. Social media algorithms fuel discord and rage. But the truth is, toxic anger isn't empowerment—it's often just unprocessed pain being projected from one hurt person to the next.

Chronic toxic anger only hurts us and pulls us farther from a conscious and peaceful planet. To break the habit loop of repeating our anger reactions, we can use regulation skills to soothe and release it in healthy ways.

But first, it's important to understand that anger doesn't always have to be fundamentally bad. Since the dawn of humanity, anger has possessed the capacity to provoke change and ensure protection. It empowers us to assert ourselves, to instigate transformation, to establish boundaries, to signal when something is wrong, and to propel our society toward a fairer, more peaceful world.

Psychologically, anger can stem from feelings of powerlessness, humiliation, or injustice. When individuals encounter situations that violate their values, expectations, or boundaries, their brains trigger the *fight, flight, or freeze* response. Anger may also be exacerbated by underlying emotions such as fear, hurt, or sadness. Additionally, learned behaviors, social norms, and cultural influences shape how individuals express and regulate their anger.

In a short-term therapy model of care, anger is not seen as a negative emotion to be suppressed. Instead, we learn to cope with and relate to anger, managing it in healthy ways to prevent destructive outcomes.

ANGER: OLD BELIEFS THAT REV UP THE AMYGDALA

Similar to the previous uncomfortable emotions we have identified, repeated narratives in our minds can intensify anger by keeping the amygdala overactivated. These thoughts often arise automatically in situations where our expectations or values are violated. Common examples include:

- "It shouldn't be this way."
- "This is not fair."
- "I am right, and they are wrong."
- "I have to change them."
- "I am responsible for punishing them."
- "I will teach them."
- "How dare they do this to me?
- "They lied."
- "This needs to change."
- "I don't deserve this."

SELF-REFLECTION WORKSHEET

What negative beliefs do you notice that add to your anger stress responses?

Which type of cognitive distortion are these beliefs?

ANGER: NEW BELIEFS THAT REV UP THE PFC

To regulate anger, we can replace these old, reactive thoughts with new, empowering beliefs that activate the prefrontal cortex (PFC). This shift allows us to process anger more logically and respond in ways that serve us better.

Five CBT tools to transform old beliefs into new beliefs:

1. Replace Old Beliefs
2. Test the Evidence
3. Repeat a Self-Compassion Mantra
4. Reframe the Narrative
5. Help or Harm

SOME HEALTHIER BELIEFS WE MIGHT ADOPT INCLUDE:

- "I will focus on what I can control and let go of what I cannot."
- "I will accept what I cannot change."
- "I will channel my anger into meaningful action."
- "I will invest my time in connecting with my community of safety where I can process my anger."
- "I cannot solve the problem when my amygdala is triggered and I don't have access to my PFC. I can wait until my nervous system calms down."
- "Karma will come back around and take care of this for me."

- "Holding onto this anger is only hurting me."
- "I will choose an empowered path to deal with this situation."
- "Two differing beliefs can exist at the same time."
- "Blame is a habit of coping with pain. I can let that go by acknowledging the complexity of human interactions and focusing on changing myself."
- "I cannot control what others say or do. I can only control how I react to that."
- "When another person suffers, it is their hurt and pain boiling over. They do not need punishment, they need help."

SELF-REFLECTION WORKSHEET

What healthy beliefs do you notice that soothe your anger stress responses?

Which tools did you use to change the cognitive distortions?

COPING SKILLS TO REGULATE ANGER

The following coping strategies can help you manage anger when it arises. By practicing them regularly, you strengthen the PFC and reduce the activation of the amygdala, making it easier to respond to anger with logic and problem solving. Using mindfulness, notice where you feel the emotion in your body. Notice which thoughts are fueling this emotion. Then choose from some of the evidence based coping skills below.

1. **Communicate the Injustice**

    Using healthy communication skills can help resolve unmet needs that trigger anger. The goal is to strike a balance between passiveness and aggressiveness by being assertive. Calm, compassionate dialogue helps defuse conflict and fosters empathy, rather than escalating it into defensiveness. Communicate your feelings and needs clearly, ensuring both parties feel heard.

2. **Accept, Change, or Leave**

    In most situations, having a sense of control over how you respond helps reduce frustration. You can break down your options into three pathways:

    - Accept the situation if it's beyond your control.
    - Change the situation by taking actionable steps.
    - Leave the situation if it's too damaging to your well-being.
    - Make a clear plan and move forward confidently, knowing you've chosen the best path.

3. **Vent then Validate**

   Anger often becomes more intense when we try to suppress or deny it. Instead, acknowledge the emotion and its underlying cause. Practice summarizing and validating your anger by reflecting on what it's trying to communicate. With others, mirroring and validating their emotions can help de-escalate tense situations and foster mutual understanding.

   Vent to yourself, or vent to others. When we are angry, stress hormones are released in the body and it can be helpful to release and express them. It can be very healing to put your anger out on paper in any creative form. In this process, we are bringing our brains back to a state of calm homeostasis. Call a trusted friend to vent and gain validation externally. Putting your anger into words—whether spoken or written—can help you process it more effectively, bringing clarity and relief.

4. **Move the Body to Complete the Stress Cycle**

   Anger prepares the body for *fight, flight, or freeze* by releasing stress hormones like adrenaline and cortisol. Physical movement helps expel this built-up energy, bringing your body back to balance. Try activities like running, dancing, or even a quick session of pushups to release tension and calm down. When you're stuck in an angry place, remember that emotions only last about 90 seconds unless we keep fueling them with cognitive stories. The next time you feel anger rising, take 90 seconds to sit with the raw sensation without adding any mental narratives. Start to move your body. Notice how the emotion begins to dissipate on its own.

5. **Make an Action Plan for Change**

   Channel your anger into meaningful, constructive actions. Injustice and inequity run rampant in our culture. Conflict and hurt feelings can run rampant in our close relationships. Activate the regions of your brain that build logic, empathy, and problem-solving skills to move toward progress and change. Empower yourself in areas where you can be an activist for change. Whether it's advocating for social justice, improving a relationship, or addressing personal frustrations, create a step-by-step action plan. Taking intentional steps helps shift your focus from feeling stuck to feeling empowered.

   Anger can also be a powerful force for creativity. Channel it into something productive, like writing, social change, or art. Many great works of art and music were born from moments of intense emotion. Using anger as fuel for creation helps transform negative energy into something meaningful and beautiful.

6. **Choose a Narrative of Empathy**

   When anger arises, it's often driven by our interpretation of others' actions. Try reframing your perspective by imagining what the other person might be going through. For example, if someone cuts you off in traffic, instead of assuming they're inconsiderate, imagine they might be rushing to an emergency. Practicing empathy helps reduce anger by softening our rigid narratives.

7. **Look at Blame Patterns and Forgive**

   Our brains are wired to jump to blame when we feel threatened. However, blame often intensifies anger rather than resolving it. Take a pause and notice when you're projecting blame onto others. Shift your focus inward, asking yourself, "What can I let go of now?" By letting go of blame, you reclaim your power to choose a healthier response. By forgiving we can choose to release feelings of resentment and pain that just hurt our nervous system. Remembering those hurtful events can prepare us for choices in the future, adding to the age-old adage we can forgive even though we don't forget. Hurt people hurt people, and we can break that cycle by setting blame down and choosing forgiveness.

8. **Lean Into Spiritual Laws and Karma**

If you believe in spiritual laws or karma, lean into these beliefs when anger feels overwhelming. Trusting that the universe will take care of injustice can provide a sense of peace and release the need for immediate retribution. What comes around, goes around and it is not our responsibly to keep everyone in check. Leaning into belief systems that make some room for some karmic punishments could be a great balm to deal with anger towards someone who has caused pain.

9. **Gold Bubble Visualization**

When you feel emotionally drained or overstimulated by your environment, try visualizing a protective gold bubble around your body. This bubble represents a boundary that keeps out negative energy and vibes while allowing you to recharge. Use this technique when entering spaces or situations that tend to provoke anger, helping you stay grounded and centered.

10. **Negotiate**

Anger can sometimes arise from unmet expectations. Instead of letting it fester, engage in a dialogue to negotiate a solution that works for both parties. Calm, clear communication about your needs and boundaries can lead to constructive outcomes. You can even negotiate between parts of yourself if internal conflict is present. Come up with mutual solutions to the problem and brainstorm how a compromise going forward will benefit both sides.

11. **Choose a Community of Safety**

    If your anger stems from experiences of discrimination or oppression, connecting with a supportive community can be incredibly healing. Sharing your experiences with people who understand and empathize can help you process anger in a safe space. Together, you can brainstorm strategies for activism, self-care, and resilience. *The Pain We Carry* by Natalie Y. Gutierrez is a great resource to address and cope with chronic discrimination.

12. **Call Someone In, Not Out**

    Instead of publicly calling someone out for problematic behavior, consider calling them in. This involves addressing the issue privately and respectfully, with the intention of fostering understanding and growth. Calling someone in can prevent defensiveness and lead to more constructive conversations. It often involves initiating a dialogue to raise awareness and promote change in a respectful and non-confrontational way.

13. **Set Boundaries**

    If certain people or situations consistently trigger your anger, it may be time to set clear boundaries. Setting boundaries helps protect your emotional well-being and reduces the likelihood of repeated frustration. Communicate your boundaries calmly and assertively, ensuring they reflect what you need to feel safe and respected. Taking back your power and controlling what and who you allow in your life can decrease anger. Say "no" to experiences or people who constantly drain your battery.

14. **Rituals**

Creating personal rituals can help you process and release anger. For example, you might go to a nearby body of water and throw rocks into it, symbolizing the release of your frustration. Writing down what makes you angry and burning the paper in a safe, controlled manner is another ritual that can provide a sense of closure. Rituals offer a structured way to acknowledge and let go of intense emotions. Research which traditions and rituals your own culture engaged in to honor grief and anger.

15. **Let Your Ego Go**

Sometimes, anger stems from a desire to be right or to prove a point. In such cases, practice letting go of the need to win or be validated. Instead, focus on the bigger picture—preserving your peace and well-being. This doesn't mean tolerating disrespect but recognizing when it's not worth the emotional toll to engage. Try to go a day without correcting anyone who says something wrong and grow within that practice of letting others be wrong.

Guided Meditation to Heal Core Anger Wounds

Find a comfortable position where your body is resting and relaxed. Scan your body to make sure all parts are supported and calm.

Take a deep breath, inhaling through your nose and exhaling through your mouth. Continue for five rounds, trying to extend and elongate the inhales and exhales as you go.

Notice any tension held in your body and invite those parts to relax. Notice any thoughts crossing your mind and bring your focus back to your breath.

Inhale white, calming light, and exhale any stress or tension. Inhale confidence, exhale doubt. Inhale peace, exhale negativity.

Now bring to mind your safest, most peaceful place in nature. Seeing it from a distance, start to step down a stone flight of stairs leading into your serene nature landscape. As you count down the steps, notice your body going even deeper into relaxation. 10, 9, 8, 7, 6, 5, 4, 3, 2.....1.

Find a comfortable seat in your favorite nature spot and absorb all the sights and sounds around you. What colors are in your nature scene? What peaceful sounds? Relaxing noises? As you relax into your scene, visualize your most Authentic, Confident Self, (ACS) walking towards you.

As you sit together, bring to mind the emotion of anger that you have been carrying. With the support of your authentic self, ask the anger how old it is. How long has it been present in your body? When was it first created? Why was it first created?

Visualize yourself going back in time to the scene where your anger was first created. How old were you? Who is involved? What situation is occurring that created this anger part in you? Who is triggering this anger?

Ask your authentic self to step forward and give you anything you need in this scene to rewrite the narrative and protect yourself from this emotional imprint of anger. What do you need to feel safe? What do you need to feel heard, seen, and taken care of? Stay in this scene absorbing as much support as needed from your healed, authentic self.

Notice what maladaptive beliefs you created as a child in this scene related to your anger. Take as much time as you need to offer your younger self wisdom, care, and new, truthful, adaptive belief systems.

Whenever you feel your time together has come to a close, hug your authentic, confident self and feel their positive energy transmitting to every cell in your body. Slowly walk back up the steps into the present, moving your fingers and toes, bringing awareness back into your body in the present.

Feel free to journal what wisdom you learned and how this early childhood scene impacts your emotional landscape today.

15 COPING SKILLS FOR ANGER	**YOUR COPING SKILLS TO MANAGE ANGER**
1. Communicate the Injustice	1. _____
2. Accept, Change or Leave	2. _____
3. Vent then Validate	3. _____
4. Complete the Stress Cycle	4. _____
5. Make a Plan of Action	5. _____
6. Choose Empathy	6. _____
7. Look at Blame Patterns and Forgive	7. _____
8. Lean into Karma	8. _____
9. Visualize Gold Bubble of Safety	9. _____
10. Negotiate	10. _____
11. Connect with Community	
12. Call In instead of Call Out	
13. Set Boundaries	
14. Engage in Rituals	
15. Let Go of Ego	

CHAPTER 4 CHEAT SHEET: BRAIN WORKOUT PLAN TO COPE WITH ANGER

- **Step into your mindful awareness.** Whenever anger arises, pause and notice what your emotional mind is thinking and feeling. Notice where it is held in your body.
- **Activate your authentic self.** From a place of compassion, choose one or more coping skills that your authentic self can offer your anger part. Choose whatever resonates with you in the moment.
- **Practice consistently.** The key to rewiring your brain is repetition. Each time you practice a coping skill, you're reinforcing healthier neural pathways that help you manage sadness more effectively.

Chapter 5: Stop Overthinking: Thought Pausing Tools

In my late twenties, I moved to a new city to start a new job while navigating a messy break up. My negative thought patterns had built up so much over the previous year that I found myself in a fog of depression. I made the choice to reach out for support and connected with a therapist.

In our initial stages of working together, she encouraged me to spend time being present in nature. So one sunny fall afternoon, I decided to lay down in my grassy backyard and look up at the passing clouds. At the time I was still overwhelmed by sadness, and I remember thinking, "This is not working, life sucks and **@#$%&!** these clouds."

The present moment can be so rich with sensory experiences, connections, beauty, and awe—but only if we are not lost in the noise of our internal worlds. Initiating coping skills from the previous chapters can be a great start to calming internal thoughts and emotions. If all of our uncomfortable emotions feel heard, seen, and dealt with, they'll be less likely to hijack our present-moment enjoyment. But what if they inevitably do?

At that moment on my lawn, I knew I needed more tools to help me manage my sadness and connect to the present moment. My overthinking habit was too loud and too persistent.

Overthinking is a common habit driven by the brain's Default Mode Network (DMN), which activates when we're not focused on a specific task. This network is responsible for mental chatter, which often spirals into worry, self-criticism, and rumination. When left unchecked, the DMN can lead to racing thoughts that disrupt our ability to focus in the present.

When I reported back to my therapist that negative thoughts were overshadowing my presence in nature, even after I used all my regulating coping skills, she gave me a life changing tool:

Thought pausing visualizations.

Thought pausing involves consciously stopping yourself in the middle of negative or spiraling thoughts to pause, let go, and refocus. My therapist pulled out a notebook and drew a number of balloons, each holding the negative thought topics that were stealing my focus from the present. She instructed me to cut the ribbons tethering the balloons filled with negative thoughts, and visualize them ascending far off into the sky. Each time they returned, I repeatedly sent them away in my imagination and over time, they quietly started to diminish.

The more I practiced noticing the intrusive thoughts and visualizing them slip away, the more present I became. Even under the clouds on my lawn in nature.

HOW THOUGHT PAUSING IMPROVES MENTAL CLARITY

Thought pausing is not about suppressing or ignoring your emotions—it's about giving yourself permission to temporarily set them aside to be more fully present in the *now*.

With regular practice, these techniques can become a powerful compliment to the skills you have already conquered in this book.

- **Reduce mental clutter:** By learning to pause persistent thoughts, you clear space in your mind for more intentional thinking.

- **Increase focus:** Thought pausing tools redirect your attention to what matters in the moment, whether that's a conversation, a task, or simply appreciating your surroundings.

- **Promote emotional balance:** When you pause racing thoughts, you give your brain a break from constant worry or over analysis, reducing emotional overwhelm.

The following thought pausing visualizations are designed to help you interrupt intrusive thought patterns and direct your focus back to the present. As you practice, remind your thoughts and emotions that they will not be ignored forever, they are simply being put aside for now, with the promise that they will be processed at a future dedicated time of your choosing.

Until then, choose a visualization below that resonates with you most, and watch your unwanted thoughts drift away like a balloon on a windy day. With practice comes strength!

CHALKBOARD VISUALIZATION

The chalkboard visualization may be helpful for short, intrusive thoughts or words that you don't want to focus on. By visualizing erasing these short phrases on the chalkboard, you can prevent them from blowing up into longer ruminations.

Picture all your racing thoughts being written on a large schoolhouse chalkboard. As soon as the board fills up with the chaotic thoughts, imagine picking up a large rectangular eraser. Watch yourself wipe the board clean, clearing away every single thought. No matter how many times the thoughts pop back up, keep erasing them until the board is empty.

Once your mental chalkboard is clear, take a deep breath and focus on the sensations of the present moment. Remind your thoughts and emotions, "I will come back to you later. Right now, I'm choosing to enjoy the present moment."

WHACK-A-MOLE VISUALIZATION

Remember the old arcade game where gopher heads pop up, and your goal is to bop them back down? Although cheesy, the Whack-a-Mole concept can be a great visualization to help with intrusive thoughts that pop up on a regular, annoying basis.

Imagine your intrusive thoughts are like those gophers. Every time an unwanted thought pops up, visualize yourself gently but firmly bopping it back down with a mallet. This playful imagery can help you stay grounded in the present moment while keeping mental distractions at bay.

> As you continue the visualization, remind your thoughts, "I will deal with you later, but for now, I'm focusing on the present."

BEACH WAVE VISUALIZATION

If you love the beach, this thought pausing tool may feel most natural to you if you find yourself in stressful situations. Picture yourself standing at the shore, where the ocean waves meet the sand. Each time an intrusive thought arises, visualize it being written in the sand at your feet. Now, invite a gentle wave to wash over the sand, wiping the thought away completely. The sand is left smooth and clean, free from the previous markings.

With every wave that washes away a thought, take a slow, deep breath. Remind yourself, "I can enjoy the peace of the present moment. My thoughts can wait."

BLACK VOID VISUALIZATION

Once I have identified negative thoughts that bring me down instead of lifting me up, I come to the conclusion that those thoughts are okay to send into an endless dark abyss. This technique can be helpful for those types of thoughts—the ones you have identified as destructive and not helpful to any part of your healing journey.

Imagine standing on a small ledge inside your mind, overlooking a vast black void that stretches infinitely. Each time a racing thought or emotion arises, watch it emerge in front of you, then see it gracefully fall into the depths of the black void. The thought disappears into the endless darkness below, leaving your mind quiet and clear. Every time it comes back up, again send it back down into the infinite abyss. As you practice this visualization, repeat to yourself, "I am safe. I can let go of these thoughts."

BALLOON POP VISUALIZATION

Balloon visualization can be helpful for people who are dealing with larger matters like family conflict, relationship stress, or any complicated issue that should be bundled up in a ball and sent away until the appropriate time.

Visualize your unwanted thoughts as being trapped inside large, colorful balloons. Once a thought is securely enclosed inside a balloon, imagine cutting the string and watching the balloon slowly drift away into the sky. As the balloon floats farther and farther away, the thought becomes smaller and smaller, until it disappears completely.

This technique is especially useful when you feel overwhelmed by persistent, intrusive thoughts. Each time you cut the string and watch a balloon float away, say to yourself, "I will return to my thoughts later. Right now, I choose to be present."

WINDSHIELD WIPERS VISUALIZATION

This one's similar to the chalk board visualization: Picture your brain space as a car windshield, with racing thoughts and emotional storms appearing as raindrops and sleet pelting the glass. Now, activate the windshield wipers, and watch as they effortlessly clear away the storm over and over. With each swipe of the wipers, the glass becomes clearer, and your focus sharpens on the present moment.

This technique provides a rhythmic, soothing visualization for pausing persistent thoughts. As you practice, remind yourself, "I will come back to these thoughts later. For now, I am enjoying what's in front of me."

CHANGE THE THOUGHT CHANNEL

Distracted by negative thoughts or large, complex matters while trying to enjoy the present? Changing the thought channel can be a quick hack to controlling your focus. Picture your mind as a television screen displaying multiple channels.

Some channels feature intrusive thoughts and heavy topics, while others show peaceful and joyful landscapes. If you find yourself stuck on a negative thought channel, imagine yourself grabbing the remote and switching to a different, more pleasant channel—perhaps one that shows a vacation memory, a peaceful nature scene, or a funny moment with friends.

Repeat this as often as necessary, and remind yourself, "I can always change the channel when I need a break from these thoughts."

PUT IT IN A JOURNAL AND CLOSE IT

Sometimes, the best way to pause racing thoughts is to acknowledge them and give them a home. This can be super helpful if you struggle with racing thoughts as you try to fall asleep each night. Grab a journal and write down whatever thoughts are running through your mind. Be as detailed as you want, knowing that once they're written down, you don't need to keep thinking about them. Once finished, physically close the journal and visualize closing the door on those thoughts until you're ready to revisit them.

Say to yourself, "These thoughts are safe in my journal. I can leave them here while I enjoy the present."

SELF-REFLECTION WORKSHEET

Developing Your Own Thought Pausing Visualizations

As you may have already noticed, thought pausing tools are personal—what works for one person may not work for another. While the techniques listed above are effective for many, you can also create your own visualizations based on your preferences and experiences. Consider the following questions to help you develop custom thought pausing methods:

Which visualization techniques resonate with you the most? Why?

What imagery or scenarios naturally make you feel calm and grounded?

Can you think of a fun or meaningful way to visualize your thoughts being paused?

What sensory imagery (sight, sound, touch) helps you feel most calm and present?

Did you notice any changes in your emotional state after using a thought pausing tool? If so, what changed?

Are there specific times of day when thought pausing feels most effective?

CHAPTER 5 CHEAT SHEET: THOUGHT PAUSING TOOLS

- Put dedicated time aside to regulate and soothe uncomfortable emotions with curiosity and compassion.

- Engage in activities that bring you into the present.

- Step into your mindful observer and notice when intrusive, unwanted thoughts are monopolizing your enjoyment of the present.

- Choose a thought pausing skill that resounds with you, and continue to practice it repeatedly if you would like to be more present.

Chapter 6: Finding and Maintaining Healthy Relationships

Brady came to my therapy office in his mid-70s. He was seeking support to help manage symptoms of depression—symptoms that had been dismissed by Brady's past doctors for decades. Beneath the surface was a history of unresolved trauma that had quietly shaped his life, leaving him with deeply ingrained negative thought patterns and maladaptive coping strategies. Brady carried a valid chip on his shoulder that showed up as hopelessness. Accompanying Brady to our first session was his wife, Patricia. Together we slowly built rapport while applying the key concepts and strategies from previous chapters of this book as our treatment plan.

Patricia continued to attend every weekly session with Brady for years. She took notes, cracked jokes, and offered helpful insights into Brady's patterns. As we progressed, the two became more and more lighthearted and joyful as they came to believe that Brady really *could* rewire his brain through mindfulness, confidence building, and healthy coping skill implementation.

Whenever Brady's amygdala jumped into action, Patricia offered him the support of her own prefrontal cortex, guiding him to choose from all the coping skills options we had processed in past sessions, in real time. Almost every coping skill listed in this book, Brady and Patricia attempted. And as he laughed, traveled, gardened, and sang with Patricia, Brady's depression shadow lifted. Two PFC's, heading toward the same goal of growth and positivity, were clearly better than one! Through kindness, clarity and calmness, Patricia always soothed Brady's *fight, flight, or freeze,* instead of triggering it.

This couple taught me that a large part of how our brains regulate can depend on the brains of those around us. Research shows that children who grow up exposed to extended trauma and violence often have larger amygdala and less access to their PFC.

If you have ever found yourself in a toxic relationship, it is easy to see that environments and relationships—past or present—can trigger our *fight, flight, or freeze* response instead of calming it. Early caregivers have great influence on how our brains develops, modeling for us how to regulate, self-soothe, and cope with stress. Or how not to.

Even though we cannot change our early childhood exposures, we can have control over the relationships we engage in as we grow and differentiate developmentally. We also can heal from past toxic relationships and interpersonal wounds through mindful awareness and the practice of new conscious, healthy interpersonal behaviors. Neuroplasticity and change are always possible in relationships.

So how do we find and cultivate healthy relationships like Brady and Patricia? First off, good news—it starts with you! Knowing your attachment style, knowing *who* your Authentic Confident Self is, and learning healthy conflict resolution skills can lead directly to more fulfilling connections.

And now that you've mastered self-awareness and built a growing toolkit of individual regulation skills, you're already well-positioned to move into interpersonal regulation awareness.

We all experience the impact of social dynamics from birth onward, and understanding how these experiences influence your relation to others can be a great catalyst for change. One way of diving deeper into your own relationship patterns is by learning more about your:

ATTACHMENT STYLE.

Attachment theory, developed by psychologists John Bowlby and Mary Ainsworth, posits that the way our early caregivers interacted with us as children impacts how we interact socially and emotionally as adults. By studying and observing children's interactions with their parents, the researchers determined four main styles of attachment: Secure, Anxious, Avoidant, and Disorganized.

Each attachment style carries with it a variety of behavior patterns that emerge when conflict and stress arise in our relationships.

SECURE ATTACHMENT

You may meet problems as they arise with healthy conflict resolution and assertive communication around your needs and feelings. You can access the front logical brain and remain regulated even in times of stress.

ANXIOUS ATTACHMENT

You may be preoccupied and perseverating on thoughts of abandonment and rejection. Small things your partner does may trigger your amygdala and the *fight, flight, or freeze* response. You overthink and are on high alert for any signs of disconnection, needing external validation of being heard, seen, and soothed.

AVOIDANT ATTACHMENT

You might shut down or move away from your partner as a coping strategy in times of discomfort. There is a struggle in tolerating vulnerability or emotional closeness when stress is present.

DISORGANIZED ATTACHMENT

You vacillate between attachment styles, inconsistent in the ways of relating to self and others. You may go back and forth between running away or clinging, showing inconsistent coping in conflict with those you care about.

Anxious or avoidant, if you tend to relate to others from an attachment style, you're not alone—and you're not stuck. With awareness and practice, it's entirely possible to build healthier, more secure patterns in your relationships.

Secure attachment behaviors can be the goal, but progress over perfection is always a helpful mindset.

HERE ARE SOME TIPS TO HELP GUIDE THAT SHIFT:

- Reflect on how your early caregivers impacted your attachment style. Both anxious and avoidant patterns often stem from unmet childhood needs. Tending to your inner child through reflection, self-compassion, and reparenting practices can be transformative.
- Identify maladaptive behaviors that are damaging your relationships and replace them with adaptive secure responses. Prevent negative cycles of conflict from happening. Look at the process of your fights, not the content.
- Take space to calm your amygdala in high stakes relationships in order to access the front brain to problem-solve and access logic. Surround yourself with people—friends, mentors, or therapists—who model secure behavior. Observing healthy relationships helps retrain your nervous system.
- Choose to respond instead of reacting. Adopt a growth mindset, regulate yourself during triggers, maintain healthy boundaries and engage in effective communication. Create a problem-solving plan together and for yourself when your attachment style hijacks the relationship.

Once we are aware of our own internal habits of relatability, we can continue to grow and engage in relationships with healthy intentions. If you are seeking deeper connections to others in your life, you can start by connecting from your ACS—not from fear, fakeness, or people-pleasing.

Next time your find yourself in a new social situation looking to build meaningful connections, remember these three words: *curiosity, commonality,* and *compliments!*

> **Curiosity:** Ask genuine questions. Show interest in others' thoughts, stories, and experiences. People feel safe and valued when they're truly heard. Prepare lists of questions you can ask those who you are engaging with. Practice the 80/20 rule with new friends or dates. Ask questions and listen 80% of the time while sharing your own thoughts 20% of the time.
>
> **Commonality:** Look for shared interests, values, or goals when meeting others. Whether it's a love for nature, food, or Taylor Swift, connection thrives where there's mutual ground. Attend event or community gatherings based on what lights you up and what you love doing.
>
> **Compliments:** Offer sincere appreciation to those around you—not just for appearances or achievements, but for who someone is. A kind word can open the door to deeper rapport.

Once you find the friends and lovers you want to invest time in, having a plan for healthy conflict resolution can be key in keeping those who you hold dear.

You may be surprised to hear that conflict in relationships is healthy and needed for growth. But as generations before us may have lacked guidance on emotional hygiene practices, so too did some lack guidance on conflict resolution skills.

We humans have a way of holding on to habits and patterns that aren't productive, and if you're like many people I've worked with over the years, you may have been taught some unhealthy extremes on the conflict resolution spectrum. Perhaps you've learned to completely shut down and turn to avoidance, or maybe you tend to engage in strong, explosive, emotional reactivity in the face of conflict.

When our amygdala triggers in relational conflict, we are being signaled that death is occurring to our social brain, which makes it very easy to swing to extreme ends of this spectrum due to habits and modeling from our past. However, we can change the way we approach conflict and choose the balanced, PFC-activated road of regulation and effective communication.

Self-compassion toward the brain's habitual response can help us understand our neurobiology and goals for change. When fight or flight takes over in an interpersonal conflict, we are flooded with chemicals that make us want to run or destroy the person next to us in battle. When our freeze state takes over, we are shut down, numb and disassociated. The goal is to instead practice ways to stay regulated, using our coping skills to activate the PFC.

The roadmap toward healthy conflict resolution can be summarized in three crucial steps:

1. Communicate effectively.
2. Create mutual understanding and respect.
3. Coregulate with healthy coping skills.

COMMUNICATE EFFECTIVELY

DEAR MAN PRACTICE:

DEAR MAN is a DBT (Dialectical Behavior Therapy) skill that helps you voice your needs while communicating effectively. The goal of this tool is to help achieve your desired outcome while maintaining positive relationships. The acronym stands for: Describe, Express, Assert, Reinforce, Mindful, Appear Confident, Negotiate.

Here's a breakdown of each step that you can practice when your next conflict arises:

D - Describe:

- Clearly and objectively describe the situation without judgment or including your emotions.
- Stick to the facts and avoid assumptions.

E - Express:

- Clearly express your feelings and opinions about the situation using "I" statements.
- Don't assume the other person understands how you feel.

A - Assert:

- Ask for what you need or want in a clear and concise manner.
- Be firm and direct when necessary.

R - Reinforce:

- Reinforce the benefits of granting your request to make it more appealing to the other person.
- Offer a win-win solution if possible.

M - Mindful:

- Stay focused on your goal and avoid getting sidetracked by the other person's reactions.
- Be mindful of your own emotional state and the other person's.

A - Appear Confident:

- Use a confident tone of voice and body language, even if you don't feel it.
- Make eye contact, stand up straight, and speak clearly.

N - Negotiate:

- Be willing to negotiate and find a compromise that works for both parties.
- Be open to alternative solutions and be flexible.

By following these steps, you can communicate your needs effectively and respectfully, increasing your chances of getting what you want while preserving your relationship.

CREATE MUTUAL UNDERSTANDING:

1. **Mirroring**

   Mirroring can be defined as accurately summarizing back the thoughts and feelings of the person sitting across from you. By reflecting back what the other person is trying to communicate, instead of preparing what you will say in response, we automatically can calm the amygdala reflex. When mirroring back another person's experience we place ourselves in their shoes, focusing on exactly what message they are trying to get across instead of planning our defense or response. Taking the time to listen and mirror back what our loved one is feeling wires our PFC while also calming the other's fight, flight or freeze.

2. **Validation**

   Giving your partner validation around their internal experience, no matter if you agree or not, automatically soothes and calms the amygdala. Normalizing how the other person if thinking and reacting to any situation provides a space for mutual connection and calming. Even if you don't see the world exactly how the other does, you can create a shared experience of validating their inner world, before moving on to share your experience, if you want to help calm the conflict.

3. **Empathy**

   Giving words of empathy for your partner's lived experience shows them you saw and heard their story. To bring the PFC back on board for all involved, try to take space to really put yourself in your partner's emotional space. Imagine what it would feel like if you were living their perception of reality. Share this with them before you take your turn explaining your side of the story.

CO-REGULATE: *THERMOMETER VISUALIZATION*

Finally, to reach your goals of engaging in healthy relationships, make a plan ahead of time to decrease emotional escalation in high stakes relationships.

Imagine your emotional escalation on a scale from 0-10 with zero being your most calm emotional state and 10 being your most triggered state. For each number on this emotional thermometer scale, choose a coping skill from previous chapters that will help deescalate you towards zero.

For example, if your partner says a hurtful comment that escalates you to a 4, have a prepared coping skill that you can use to bring you down to a 2. Breathing, venting, or mirroring could be some possible options. Learn what actions help your partner de-escalate as well.

Plan with your partner so you know how to lower each number on the escalation scale. What skills help your partner deescalate in conflict?

What skills help you deescalate in conflict? How can you work as a team to bring both nervous systems to a calmer state?

SELF-REFLECTION WORKSHEET

What is your attachment style?

What goals can you set for yourself to build heathier attachments to self and other?

What shared activities can you do with others that highlight your Authentic Confident Self?

Where can you spend time socially with people who may share your values, strengths, and hobbies?

How can you show up interpersonally from your ACS instead of from your fear parts?

What strengths can you bring into your relationships?

CHAPTER 6 CHEAT SHEET: FINDING AND MAINTAINING HEALTHY RELATIONSHIPS

- Understand and reflect on your attachment style.
- Practice new skills and behaviors to move towards secure, assertive communication and attachment style.
- Find and make friends and possible partners through curiosity, common interests, and compliments.
- Resolve conflict in your high stake's relationships with assertive communication, coping skills, and a premade collaborative plan.

Chapter 7: Brain Mood Boosts!

We're on the home stretch, and if you've made it this far, you've come a long way already! So far, we've explored how to practice mindful awareness, nurture our Authentic Confident Self, regulate uncomfortable emotions in healthy ways, and cultivate thriving relationships by partnering to encourage Secure Attachment within a shared space of support.

All of these long-term strategies will help build new neural pathways over time and transform the way you move through the complex emotional landscape of modern life.

Still, we all know that sometimes the brain needs a quick boost in the moment. Picture these final techniques as your go-to 'cheat sheet' for up-regulating the four neurotransmitters responsible for stabilizing your mental state—dopamine, oxytocin, serotonin, and endorphins. Each of these chemicals plays a unique role in shaping your mood, motivation, and sense of well-being, and the following techniques are designed to help you tap into their unique power.

By incorporating simple daily habits that stimulate these neurotransmitters, you can enhance your mental and emotional balance in the moment while promoting long-term happiness. In other words, these strategies work as quick, science-backed ways to feel better and strengthen your brain's reward and regulation systems.

DOPAMINE: THE REWARD CHEMICAL

If you remember our "crash course" from Chapter 1, you know that dopamine is often associated with the brain's reward system. It drives our motivation, fuels our desire for achievement, and provides a sense of pleasure when we accomplish something. Whether you're finishing a small task, anticipating a reward, or simply indulging in an enjoyable activity, dopamine is the chemical that makes you feel good about it.

Try some of these practical ways to naturally increase dopamine:
Expectation for Reward

Did you know that dopamine isn't just released when you receive a reward—it's actually triggered in anticipation of it? This is why the act of waiting for something enjoyable can feel so exciting. Whether it's looking forward to a night out, planning a weekend trip, or even anticipating a delicious meal, this expectation amplifies dopamine release, increasing motivation and excitement.

Quick Tip:

Use this science to your advantage by booking enjoyable activities after stressful work commitments. Knowing that something fun is coming up can make it easier to push through challenging tasks. For example, schedule a coffee date with a friend or plan a reward after completing a big project. Plan a reward that will light you up!

Introversion vs. Extroversion and Dopamine

Interestingly, research shows that extroverts tend to have higher baseline dopamine activity, which explains why they often seek external stimulation, such as social interactions or novel experiences. On the other hand, introverts exhibit a more subdued dopamine response to external stimuli, meaning they may derive pleasure more from internal rewards, such as reflection, creativity, or quiet hobbies.

Quick Tip:
If you're introverted, focus on activities that bring you joy internally, like reading, journaling, or engaging in a solo creative project. If you're extroverted, plan social outings or group activities that give your brain the dopamine boost it craves.

Cold Therapy

Cold exposure has recently gained popularity for its dopamine-boosting effects. Techniques such as cold showers or ice baths can trigger a sustained release of dopamine, improving mood and motivation. Pioneered by Wim Hof and supported by neuroscientists like Andrew Huberman, cold therapy offers a natural, long-lasting boost without the crash associated with substances like caffeine or alcohol.

Quick Tip:
Start small—try ending your shower with 10-30 seconds of cold water. As uncomfortable as it may seem, the post-shower dopamine surge can leave you feeling exhilarated and energized.

Sex

Few things trigger dopamine as reliably as sex. This activity activates the brain's reward system, reinforcing behaviors essential for survival and reproduction. Sexual activity heightens dopamine release, increasing pleasure and connection.

Quick Tip:

Plan date nights that excite you. The simple act of looking forward to these moments can give you a dopamine boost well before they happen.

Social Media: The Dopamine Trap

Social media platforms are designed to hijack your brain's reward system by delivering unpredictable rewards—likes, comments, and shares trigger dopamine spikes, making scrolling addictive. This same mechanism explains why people can become addicted to unreliable romantic partners who create a similar cycle of anticipation and uncertainty.

Quick Tip:

Set boundaries around social media use. Instead of relying on external validation, practice internal validation by acknowledging your own worth. Use thought pausing tools to interrupt compulsive scrolling and return to the present moment. Optimize your social media accounts to follow users who boost you up, inspire, and reflect back things that bring you joy. Follow accounts that mirror things you love. Cute puppy posts like those from @famaousmisspeaches are ones that give me a daily boost!

Anticipating a Vacation or New Experience

Just thinking about a future vacation or adventure can trigger dopamine release. The anticipation of exploring new places or trying new activities lights up the brain's pleasure centers, increasing motivation and excitement.

Quick Tip:

Even if you can't plan a trip right now, take a moment to daydream about future adventures. Visualizing yourself in a new place can give you a small dopamine boost.

Watching Your Favorite Sports Team Win

When you're emotionally invested in a sports team, watching them win can trigger a significant dopamine surge. (Go Bills!) This is partly due to mirror neurons, which allow us to experience others' emotions as if they were our own. Cheering with a community of fans also enhances the reward system by creating a sense of connection and shared purpose.

Quick Tip:

Next time your favorite team is playing, make an event out of it—invite friends over, wear team colors, and fully immerse yourself in the experience. Even if your team loses, the sense of community can still provide a dopamine boost.

Yoga Nidra Meditation

Yoga Nidra, often described as yogic sleep, promotes deep relaxation while keeping the mind consciously aware. This practice has been shown to increase dopamine levels by helping the brain enter a restorative state, enhancing mood and reducing stress.

Quick Tip: Look for a guided Yoga Nidra session online or attend a local class. Even a 20-minute session can leave you feeling refreshed and mentally balanced.

Cluster Tasks

Clustering tasks involves grouping similar activities together to improve focus and efficiency. Breaking up tasks into small, manageable chunks with rewards in between can boost dopamine levels by providing a sense of accomplishment with each completed step.

Quick Tip:

At the start of your day, create a to-do list with tasks grouped by type. After completing a cluster, take a short break or treat yourself to something enjoyable to keep your dopamine levels high.

Binge-Watching Your Favorite Show:

Great news for Andy Cohen — Yes, binge-watching your favorite reality show can boost dopamine—especially when you're emotionally invested in the characters and plot. Shows with unpredictable twists or reality TV that lets you vicariously experience drama, success, or humor can trigger a steady release of dopamine.

Quick Tip:

Use binge-watching as a reward for completing tasks or winding down at the end of the day. Just be mindful of moderation—too much screen time can disrupt sleep and mood.

OXYTOCIN: THE LOVE CHEMICAL

Oxytocin is often called the "bonding hormone" or "love chemical" because it plays a vital role in building trust, emotional connection, and intimacy. This neurotransmitter is released during moments of physical touch, emotional bonding, and even shared positive experiences. Boosting oxytocin can enhance your relationships, reduce stress, and promote overall well-being.

Try some of these practical ways to naturally increase oxytocin:

20-Second Hug

Did you know that a simple 20-second hug can significantly increase oxytocin levels? Physical touch, when consensual and comfortable, triggers the release of oxytocin, fostering feelings of trust, warmth, and connection.

Quick Tip:

Find opportunities for longer hugs with loved ones, friends, or even your pet (if they're patient enough). A hug lasting at least 20 seconds provides an oxytocin surge, improving mood and reducing stress.

Playing with Cute Puppies or Animals

Spending time with animals—especially puppies—can be a quick and effective way to boost oxytocin. The playful and affectionate nature of pets stimulates oxytocin release, making us feel happier and more connected.

Quick Tip:

If you don't have a pet, consider visiting a friend who does or volunteering at a local animal shelter. Even brief interactions with animals can lift your spirits and reduce stress.

Eye Contact

Eye contact plays a crucial role in building trust and emotional connection. Holding someone's gaze during a conversation can signal safety and empathy, triggering oxytocin release. This is why eye contact is often used as a tool in counseling and therapy to foster a sense of being seen and understood.

Quick Tip:

Practice mindful eye contact in conversations with people you trust. However, if you're neurodivergent and find eye contact uncomfortable or stressful, skip this tip and focus on other oxytocin-boosting techniques that suit your needs.

Hand Holding

Something as simple as holding hands can stimulate oxytocin production. Whether it's with a romantic partner, a friend, or a family member, hand holding creates a sense of closeness and comfort.

Quick Tip:

When feeling anxious or disconnected, reach out for a loved one's hand. The warmth and pressure of this physical connection can help calm your nervous system and boost oxytocin.

Snuggling and Comfort

Snuggling—whether with a partner, a child, or even a pet—can release oxytocin and promote feelings of safety and affection. The physical touch involved in snuggling activates sensory receptors that stimulate oxytocin production.

Quick Tip:

Create a cozy environment with soft pillows, blankets, or anything that makes you feel physically comfortable. Whether alone or with someone else, engaging in sensory comfort can be a powerful way to soothe your nervous system.

Favorite Books, Shows, or Movies

Storytelling has been shown to increase oxytocin and promote emotional connection. When we get lost in a great book or become emotionally invested in a show or movie, our brains release oxytocin, fostering empathy and reducing stress.

Quick Tip:

Pick a favorite book, show, or movie that brings you joy and comfort. Even just 30 minutes of storytelling immersion can lift your mood and provide an oxytocin boost.

Intimacy and Trust (Gossip)

Gossiping isn't always a negative thing—when done with trust and empathy, it can actually increase oxytocin by fostering connection. Sharing personal experiences, emotions, or opinions in a trusted setting strengthens social bonds and releases oxytocin.

Quick Tip:

Instead of gossiping negatively, use this time to confide in someone you trust. Sharing your thoughts and receiving empathy can create a quick oxytocin boost. Live vicariously through others' drama with reality TV shows—and let the drama stay there!

Confirmation Bias and Validation

When someone confirms your beliefs or validates your experiences, your brain releases oxytocin. This is one reason why we feel so good when we connect with like-minded individuals—it strengthens our sense of belonging and trust.

Quick Tip:
Find a friend or a community that shares your interests or beliefs. Engaging in conversations where you feel heard and understood can enhance oxytocin levels.

Cultivating Empathy

Empathy is a powerful driver of oxytocin release. When we listen to and genuinely care for others, our brains reward us by releasing oxytocin, encouraging more empathetic behavior. Empathy also strengthens social bonds and promotes emotional well-being.

Quick Tip:
Practice active listening in your daily interactions. Whether it's a friend venting or a family member sharing their day, offering your full attention can foster empathy and boost oxytocin for both of you.

SEROTONIN: THE MOOD STABILIZER

Serotonin is crucial for mood regulation, emotional stability, and overall mental well-being. Low serotonin levels are often linked to anxiety, depression, and irritability, while balanced serotonin levels promote calmness, happiness, and emotional resilience.

Here are some natural ways to increase serotonin levels:

Sunlight Exposure

Sunlight plays a key role in serotonin synthesis. When UV rays hit your skin, they trigger a process that increases serotonin production in the brain. Regular sunlight exposure helps regulate your mood, sleep-wake cycles, and overall emotional health.

> **Quick Tip:**
>
> Spend at least 15-20 minutes outside every day, preferably in the morning. If you live in a place with limited sunlight, consider investing in a UV light therapy lamp.

Gut Health

Did you know that the majority of serotonin is produced in your gut? A healthy gut microbiome supports serotonin synthesis, which directly impacts your mood and mental well-being. Foods rich in probiotics and prebiotics promote gut health and, in turn, serotonin production.

> **Quick Tip:**
>
> Incorporate fermented foods like yogurt, kefir, sauerkraut, and kimchi into your diet. Also, aim for a balanced diet rich

in protein, fiber, fruits, and vegetables to support a healthy gut.

Eating Foods Rich in Tryptophan

Tryptophan is an essential amino acid that plays a crucial role in serotonin production. When consumed, tryptophan is transported to the brain, where it's converted into serotonin with the help of specific enzymes. Foods high in tryptophan include poultry, dairy products, eggs, nuts, seeds, tofu, and grains like oats and quinoa.

Quick Tip:

Incorporate tryptophan-rich foods into your meals. Pair them with complex carbohydrates (like whole grains or vegetables) to help facilitate the transport of tryptophan to the brain.

Sleep Cycles

Good sleep hygiene is vital for maintaining healthy serotonin levels. Serotonin not only plays a role in regulating mood but is also a precursor to melatonin, the hormone that governs sleep. Disrupted or insufficient sleep can negatively impact serotonin synthesis, leading to mood disturbances.

Quick Tip:

Prioritize getting 7-9 hours of sleep each night. Create a relaxing bedtime routine with warm baths, relaxing teas, or smells, keep your sleep environment comfortable, and maintain a consistent sleep schedule. Avoid napping throughout the day. Try to get 10-30 minutes of early morning sun to help your circadian rhythms stay on track.

Laughing and Making Others Laugh

Laughter is not only a great way to release tension but also a proven method to increase serotonin. Sharing humor with others, whether by telling jokes or enjoying a funny show, boosts serotonin by promoting positive social interactions and reducing stress.

Quick Tip:

Make laughter a part of your daily routine. Watch a funny show, share memes with friends, or tell a good joke. Even attempting to make others laugh can give you a serotonin boost.

Exercise

Physical activity is one of the most effective ways to boost serotonin levels. Exercise increases the availability of tryptophan, the amino acid that serves as a precursor for serotonin production. Additionally, exercise improves mood by releasing endorphins, creating a double benefit.

Quick Tip:

Incorporate moderate exercise into your routine, whether it's a brisk walk, yoga, or strength training. Aim for 20-30 minutes a day, and choose activities you enjoy to make it easier to stick with.

Sound Baths

Sound baths, where participants are immersed in therapeutic sound vibrations from instruments like singing bowls or gongs, have been linked to increased serotonin levels. The soothing sounds promote deep relaxation and reduce stress, creating a fertile environment for serotonin production.

Quick Tip:

Attend a local sound bath session or find guided sound bath meditations online. Even 10-20 minutes of intentional listening can promote a sense of calm and elevate your mood.

Recalling Good Memories

Recalling positive past experiences can increase serotonin levels by promoting feelings of gratitude and happiness. This practice shifts your focus away from stressors and encourages a more positive outlook.

Quick Tip:

Keep a journal of happy memories or achievements. When feeling down, take a few moments to read through your entries and relive those moments.

ENDORPHINS: THE PAIN KILLER

Endorphins are the body's natural pain relievers. Released during physical activity, laughter, and certain pleasurable experiences, endorphins create feelings of euphoria and help reduce stress. Endorphins not only block pain but also enhance your overall sense of well-being.

Try some of these practical ways to naturally increase endorphins:
Flow State
Being fully immersed in an activity, also known as being in a flow state, triggers the release of endorphins. Flow occurs when you're deeply focused on a task that challenges you just enough to keep you engaged but not so much that it causes anxiety. Activities like sports, creative projects, or problem-solving can induce this state.

> **Quick Tip:**
> Identify activities that naturally put you in a flow state, whether it's painting, playing music, or engaging in a sport. Set aside dedicated time for these activities each week.

Massage
Massage therapy has been shown to stimulate endorphin release, leading to reduced pain and increased relaxation. The pressure applied during a massage activates sensory receptors, which signal the brain to produce endorphins.

> **Quick Tip:**
> Schedule a professional massage or practice self-massage techniques at home. Even a brief shoulder or foot massage can provide relief and elevate your mood.

Laughing

Laughter triggers the release of both dopamine and endorphins, making it one of the easiest and most enjoyable ways to feel better. Studies show that laughter can increase pain tolerance by up to 15% due to the endorphin rush it creates.

Quick Tip:

Before a stressful event or meeting, take a few minutes to watch a funny video or read something humorous. Not only will it help relax you, but it may also improve your performance by boosting your mood.

Dancing and Music

Dancing, especially when combined with music you enjoy, is a powerful way to boost endorphins. The rhythmic movement and coordination with music stimulate endorphin production while also enhancing dopamine release.

Quick Tip:

Put on your favorite upbeat playlist and dance around your room for 10-15 minutes. Not only will it lift your spirits, but it will also give you a fun workout.

Dark Chocolate

Dark chocolate contains compounds that stimulate the release of endorphins. The rich taste and indulgent experience of eating dark chocolate can also trigger dopamine release, providing a double boost of feel-good chemicals.

Quick Tip:

Enjoy a small piece of high-quality dark chocolate (at least 70% cocoa) as a treat during your day.

UV Light Exposure

UV light exposure, whether from the sun or a light therapy box, has been shown to increase the release of beta-endorphins, which are associated with improved mood and reduced pain sensitivity. This is one reason why many people feel happier after spending time in the sun.

Quick Tip:

Whenever possible, spend time outdoors during daylight hours. If you're in a cold or dark climate, consider investing in a light therapy lamp to simulate natural sunlight.

CHAPTER 7 CHEAT SHEET: BRAIN MOOD BOOSTS

- Make an outline of a typical day based on your schedule. Pencil in specific actions throughout the day that will boost your four "feel good" chemicals.
- Write up a quick-tip cheat sheet and use mindfulness to choose those actions whenever you are in a crunch and needing a boost of dopamine, oxytocin, serotonin, or endorphins.
- Reward yourself throughout the stressful responsibility of life with as many as these quick-tip actions as you can.

The 21-Day Accountability Journal

You've made it to the finish line!

After giving yourself a huge congratulations on how far you've come, it's time for one final step to make a habit of putting all these powerful tools into regular practice. Remember, *neurons that fire together, wire together.* The goal of your short-term therapy program is not just gathering strategies, but to come away with a roadmap toward *changing your brain* in the long run.

Consistency is key, and we want to take steps toward making these strategies habitual in your everyday life. So without further ado... welcome to your 21-Day Accountability Journal!

Here is where you'll begin to actively apply everything you've learned so far—mindfulness, emotional regulation, confidence-building, and boosting feel-good chemicals—into a consistent daily practice. This journal is designed to guide you through a 21-day process of self-awareness, habit formation, and personal growth. Each day includes structured prompts to help you reflect on your progress, track your emotions, and reinforce those brand-new neural pathways.

By committing to this practice for 21 days, you'll strengthen your brain's ability to manage stress, increase focus, and cultivate positive emotional states.

The goal isn't perfection—it's about showing up every day and being intentional in your efforts to rewire your brain for better well-being.

How to Use This Journal

Daily Prompts

Each day you'll complete six key prompts that focus on:

- Practicing mindfulness.
- Embodying your Authentic Confident Self.
- Reinforcing new, positive beliefs.
- Using coping skills to regulate negative emotions.
- Engaging in healthy relationship patterns.
- Boosting your brain's feel-good chemicals.

End-of-Journal Reflection

After completing 21 days, you'll review your progress by answering prompts designed to help you notice changes in your thoughts, emotions, and overall well-being. This final reflection will serve as encouragement to continue your new habits beyond the 21-day period.

HERE IS A BREAKDOWN OF EACH JOURNAL EXERCISE PROMPT

Ways I Practiced Mindful Awareness

Mindfulness is about bringing your attention to the present moment without judgment. Think about moments in your day where you consciously paused, noticed your surroundings, or focused on your breath.

Example:

"I practiced mindful breathing for 5 minutes in the morning. I noticed my thoughts wandering during a meeting, and I brought my attention back to my breath."

Ways I Practiced Being My Authentic Confident Self

Being your authentic self means showing up as you are, without filtering or masking your identity. Confidence comes from consistently aligning your actions with your values.

Example:

"I spoke up during the team meeting and shared my opinion, even though I felt nervous. I reminded myself that my perspective is valid."

New Beliefs I Wired

Every time you replace an old, negative belief with a new, empowering one, you're rewiring your brain. Reflect on which beliefs you practiced today.

Example:

"I repeated the belief: 'I am capable of handling challenges.' I replaced thoughts of self-doubt with this belief throughout the day."

Coping Skills I Engaged in to Regulate Uncomfortable Emotions

Think about moments when you felt overwhelmed or stressed and used a coping skill to manage your emotions. This could be a thought pausing tool, deep breathing, or reaching out for support.

Example:

"When I felt anxious during the afternoon, I used the chalkboard visualization to clear my mind. I also took a short walk outside to calm down."

Ways I Engaged in Healthy Relationships

Reflect on ways that you interacted with others today. Notice when you communicated effectively or worked through a conflict with a loved one in ways you felt proud of.

Example:

"Today I helped my partner calm down when they were upset. I listened actively and mirrored back their pain."

Feel-Good Chemicals That I Wired

Identify activities that helped boost dopamine, oxytocin, serotonin, or endorphins. These could include exercise, social connection, laughter, or completing a task.

Example:

"I boosted dopamine by completing a small task I had been procrastinating on. I increased serotonin by spending 15 minutes in the sunlight."

DAY 1:

Ways I Practiced Mindful Awareness:

Ways I Practiced Being My Authentic Confident Self:

New Beliefs I Wired:

Coping Skills I Used to Regulate Uncomfortable Emotions:

Ways I Engaged in Healthy Relationships:

Feel-Good Chemicals I Wired:

DAY 2:

Ways I Practiced Mindful Awareness:

Ways I Practiced Being My Authentic Confident Self:

New Beliefs I Wired:

Coping Skills I Used to Regulate Uncomfortable Emotions:

Ways I Engaged in Healthy Relationships:

Feel-Good Chemicals I Wired:

DAY 3:

Ways I Practiced Mindful Awareness:

Ways I Practiced Being My Authentic Confident Self:

New Beliefs I Wired:

Coping Skills I Used to Regulate Uncomfortable Emotions:

Ways I engaged in Healthy Relationships:

Feel-Good Chemicals I Wired:

DAY 4:

Ways I Practiced Mindful Awareness:

Ways I Practiced Being My Authentic Confident Self:

New Beliefs I Wired:

Coping Skills I Used to Regulate Uncomfortable Emotions:

Ways I engaged in Healthy Relationships:

Feel-Good Chemicals I Wired:

DAY 5:

Ways I Practiced Mindful Awareness:

Ways I Practiced Being My Authentic Confident Self:

New Beliefs I Wired:

Coping Skills I Used to Regulate Uncomfortable Emotions:

Ways I engaged in Healthy Relationships:

Feel-Good Chemicals I Wired:

DAY 6:

Ways I Practiced Mindful Awareness:

Ways I Practiced Being My Authentic Confident Self:

New Beliefs I Wired:

Coping Skills I Used to Regulate Uncomfortable Emotions:

Ways I engaged in Healthy Relationships:

Feel-Good Chemicals I Wired:

DAY 7:

Ways I Practiced Mindful Awareness:

Ways I Practiced Being My Authentic Confident Self:

New Beliefs I Wired:

Coping Skills I Used to Regulate Uncomfortable Emotions:

Ways I engaged in Healthy Relationships:

Feel-Good Chemicals I Wired:

DAY 8:

Ways I Practiced Mindful Awareness:

Ways I Practiced Being My Authentic Confident Self:

New Beliefs I Wired:

Coping Skills I Used to Regulate Uncomfortable Emotions:

Ways I engaged in Healthy Relationships:

Feel-Good Chemicals I Wired:

DAY 9:

~

Ways I Practiced Mindful Awareness:

Ways I Practiced Being My Authentic Confident Self:

New Beliefs I Wired:

Coping Skills I Used to Regulate Uncomfortable Emotions:

Ways I engaged in Healthy Relationships:

Feel-Good Chemicals I Wired:

DAY 10:

∽

Ways I Practiced Mindful Awareness:

Ways I Practiced Being My Authentic Confident Self:

New Beliefs I Wired:

Coping Skills I Used to Regulate Uncomfortable Emotions:

Ways I engaged in Healthy Relationships:

Feel-Good Chemicals I Wired:

DAY 11:

∽

Ways I Practiced Mindful Awareness:

Ways I Practiced Being My Authentic Confident Self:

New Beliefs I Wired:

Coping Skills I Used to Regulate Uncomfortable Emotions:

Ways I engaged in Healthy Relationships:

Feel-Good Chemicals I Wired:

DAY 12:

Ways I Practiced Mindful Awareness:

Ways I Practiced Being My Authentic Confident Self:

New Beliefs I Wired:

Coping Skills I Used to Regulate Uncomfortable Emotions:

Ways I engaged in Healthy Relationships:

Feel-Good Chemicals I Wired:

DAY 13:

Ways I Practiced Mindful Awareness:

Ways I Practiced Being My Authentic Confident Self:

New Beliefs I Wired:

Coping Skills I Used to Regulate Uncomfortable Emotions:

Ways I engaged in Healthy Relationships:

Feel-Good Chemicals I Wired:

DAY 14:

Ways I Practiced Mindful Awareness:

Ways I Practiced Being My Authentic Confident Self:

New Beliefs I Wired:

Coping Skills I Used to Regulate Uncomfortable Emotions:

Ways I engaged in Healthy Relationships:

Feel-Good Chemicals I Wired:

DAY 15:

Ways I Practiced Mindful Awareness:

Ways I Practiced Being My Authentic Confident Self:

New Beliefs I Wired:

Coping Skills I Used to Regulate Uncomfortable Emotions:

Ways I engaged in Healthy Relationships:

Feel-Good Chemicals I Wired:

DAY 16:

Ways I Practiced Mindful Awareness:

Ways I Practiced Being My Authentic Confident Self:

New Beliefs I Wired:

Coping Skills I Used to Regulate Uncomfortable Emotions:

Ways I engaged in Healthy Relationships:

Feel-Good Chemicals I Wired:

DAY 17:

Ways I Practiced Mindful Awareness:

Ways I Practiced Being My Authentic Confident Self:

New Beliefs I Wired:

Coping Skills I Used to Regulate Uncomfortable Emotions:

Ways I engaged in Healthy Relationships:

Feel-Good Chemicals I Wired:

DAY 18:

Ways I Practiced Mindful Awareness:

Ways I Practiced Being My Authentic Confident Self:

New Beliefs I Wired:

Coping Skills I Used to Regulate Uncomfortable Emotions:

Ways I engaged in Healthy Relationships:

Feel-Good Chemicals I Wired:

DAY 19:

∼

Ways I Practiced Mindful Awareness:

Ways I Practiced Being My Authentic Confident Self:

New Beliefs I Wired:

Coping Skills I Used to Regulate Uncomfortable Emotions:

Ways I engaged in Healthy Relationships:

Feel-Good Chemicals I Wired:

DAY 20:

Ways I Practiced Mindful Awareness:

Ways I Practiced Being My Authentic Confident Self:

New Beliefs I Wired:

Coping Skills I Used to Regulate Uncomfortable Emotions:

Ways I engaged in Healthy Relationships:

Feel-Good Chemicals I Wired:

DAY 21:

Ways I Practiced Mindful Awareness:

Ways I Practiced Being My Authentic Confident Self:

New Beliefs I Wired:

Coping Skills I Used to Regulate Uncomfortable Emotions:

Ways I engaged in Healthy Relationships:

Feel-Good Chemicals I Wired:

End-of-Journal Reflection: Noticing Changes in Thoughts, Emotions, and Overall Well-Being

Congratulations on completing your 21-day brain workout plan! Taking the time to consistently practice mindfulness, build confidence, regulate emotions, and boost your brain's feel-good chemicals is a significant achievement. Now, let's take a moment to reflect on your journey, notice the changes you've experienced, and consider how you can continue these habits beyond the 21 days.

REFLECTION PROMPTS

What thoughts are you noticing now compared to the start of the journal?

Reflect on whether your thought patterns have changed. Are your thoughts more balanced or supportive? Have you noticed a reduction in negative or intrusive thinking?

Example:

"At the start of the journal, I noticed a lot of self-doubt and critical thoughts. Now, I'm more aware of these patterns and can replace them with positive beliefs. My mind feels calmer, and I can redirect my focus more easily."

What emotions are you noticing now compared to the start of the journal?

Take a moment to assess how your emotional landscape has shifted. Are you experiencing more positive emotions? Are you better able to manage difficult emotions when they arise?

Example:

"I've noticed that I feel more grounded and less overwhelmed. When anxiety arises, I can acknowledge it without getting caught up in it. I've also felt more moments of joy and gratitude."

Where do you notice your focus and attention being pulled to now? Reflect on whether your ability to stay present has improved. Are you more aware of when your mind starts to wander? Have you found it easier to bring your attention back to the present?

Example:

"I'm more mindful throughout the day. I catch myself when my thoughts drift and gently bring my focus back to the present. I've noticed I can stay engaged in conversations and tasks more easily."

What changes have you noticed in your overall well-being?

Think about any physical, mental, or emotional changes you've experienced. This could include improved sleep, increased energy, or a greater sense of calm and clarity.

Example:

"My overall mood has improved—I feel more optimistic and less reactive to stress. I've also noticed that I sleep better and wake up feeling more refreshed."

Which practices or habits have been the most helpful for you? Why? Identify the specific techniques or habits that made the biggest difference in your well-being. This reflection can help you decide which habits to continue beyond the 21 days.

Example:

"The morning mindfulness practice has been incredibly helpful in setting a calm tone for my day. I also found the gratitude coping skills in the evening really boosted my mood and helped me sleep better."

By completing this 21-day journal, you've taken an important step toward improving your mental and emotional well-being. You've built habits that strengthen your brain, foster resilience, and enhance your overall quality of life. Whether you continue journaling daily or simply integrate a few key practices into your routine, know that every small effort counts.

You have the tools. You have the awareness. And most importantly, you have the power to continue growing into the best version of yourself.

Keep going, stay curious, and be proud of the work you've done—your brain is thanking you for it!

References

Kabat-Zinn, J. (1994). Wherever you go there you are. Hyperion.

Hölzel, B. K., Carmody, J., Vangel, M., Congleton, C., Yerramsetti, S. M., Gard, T., & Lazar, S. W. (2011). Mindfulness practice leads to increases in regional brain gray matter density. *Psychiatry Research: Neuroimaging*, 191(1), 36-43

Gutierrez, N. Y. (2018). The pain we carry: A father's meditation on loss and hope. Resource Publications

Peters, J., & Büchel, C. (2010). The neural mechanisms of intertemporal decision-making: understanding variability. Trends in Cognitive Sciences, 14(7), 354–361. https://doi.org/10.1016/j.tics.2010.05.004

QBI. (n.d.). Depression and the brain. Queensland Brain Institute. Retrieved from https://qbi.uq.edu.au/brain/brain-diseases/depression/depression-and-brain

National Geographic. (2011, October 20). Teenage Brains. https://www.nationalgeographic.com/magazine/2011/10/teenage-brains/

Tolle, E. (1999). The power of now: A guide to spiritual enlightenment. New World Library.

Hofmann, S. G., Grossman, P., & Hinton, D. E. (2011). Loving-kindness and compassion meditation: Potential for psychological interventions. Clinical Psychology Review, 31(7), 1126–1132. https://doi.org/10.1016/j.cpr.2011.07.003

Kabat-Zinn, J. (2005). Coming to our senses: Healing ourselves and the world through mindfulness. Hyperion.

Levine, P. A. (1997). Waking the tiger: Healing trauma. North Atlantic Books.

Paul, M. (1993). Healing your aloneness: Finding love and wholeness through your inner child. New World Library.

McKay, M., Wood, J. C., & Brantley, J. (2007). The dialectical behavior therapy skills workbook: Practical DBT exercises for learning mindfulness, interpersonal effectiveness, emotion regulation, and distress tolerance. New Harbinger Publications.

Burns, D. D. (2019). Feeling good: The new mood therapy. HarperCollins.

Koechlin, E., & Summerfield, C. (2007). An information theoretical approach to prefrontal executive function. Trends in Cognitive Sciences, 11(6), 229–235. https://doi.org/10.1016/j.tics.2007.04.005

Kirsch, I., & Lynn, S. J. (1995). Altered states of hypnosis: Changes in the theoretical landscape. American Psychologist, 50(10), 846–858. https://doi.org/10.1037/0003-066X.50.10.846

Craig, G. (2011). The EFT manual (3rd ed.). Energy Psychology Press.

Menanno, J. (2018). Secure love: Building happy and lasting relationships. CreateSpace Independent Publishing Platform.

Chmurzyńska, A. (2006). The multigene family of fatty acid-binding proteins (FABPs): Function, structure and polymorphism. Journal of Applied Genetics, 47(1), 39–48.

Nhat Hanh, T. (2001). Anger: Wisdom for cooling the flames. Riverhead Books.

Kessler, D. (2019). Finding meaning: The sixth stage of grief. Scribner.

Gaddis, J. (2018). Getting to zero: How to work through conflict in your high stakes relationships. Lioncrest Publishing.

Fisher, H. (1994). Anatomy of Love: A Natural History of Mating, Marriage, and Why We Stray. Paperback edition. Random House.

Brown, B. (Year). Rising Strong: How the Ability to Reset Transforms the Way We Live, Love, Parent, and Lead. Random House.

Brown, a. m. (n.d.). We Will Not Cancel Us: And Other Dreams of Transformative Justice.

Storytelling increases oxytocin and positive emotions and decreases cortisol and pain in hospitalized children: June 2021Proceedings of the National Academy of Sciences 118(22): e2018409118Guilherme Brockington Universidade Federal de São PauloAna Paula Gomes Moreira, Maria Stephani Buso, Sérgio Gomes da Silva, Fundação Cristiano Varella

Dopamine, Oxytocin, Serotonin, Endorphin Research References:

Schultz, W. (2016). Dopamine reward prediction error coding. Dialogues in Clinical Neuroscience, 18(1), 23–32.

Depue, R. A., & Collins, P. F. (1999). Neurobiology of the structure of personality: Dopamine, facilitation of incentive motivation, and extraversion. Behavioral and Brain Sciences, 22(3), 491–517. https://doi.org/10.1017/S0140525X99002046

Hof, W., & Kox, M. (2016). Voluntary activation of the sympathetic nervous system and attenuation of the innate immune response in humans. Proceedings of the National Academy of Sciences, 113(35), 201520780. https://doi.org/10.1073/pnas.1605410113

Volkow, N. D., Wang, G. J., Baler, R. D., & Volkow, N. D. (2011). Reward, dopamine and the control of food intake: Implications for obesity. Trends in Cognitive Sciences, 15(1), 37–46. https://doi.org/10.1016/j.tics.2010.11.001

Kuss, D. J., & Griffiths, M. D. (2017). Social networking sites and addiction: Ten lessons learned. International Journal of Environmental Research and Public Health, 14(3), 311. https://doi.org/10.3390/ijerph14030311

Knutson, B., & Greer, S. M. (2008). Anticipatory affect: Neural correlates and consequences for choice. Philosophical Transactions of the Royal Society B: Biological Sciences, 363(1511), 3771–3786. https://doi.org/10.1098/rstb.2008.0155

Coates, D., & Herbert, J. (2008). Endogenous steroids and financial risk taking on a London trading floor. Proceedings of the National Academy of Sciences, 105(16), 6167–6172. https://doi.org/10.1073/pnas.0704025105

Cahn, B. R., & Polich, J. (2006). Meditation states and traits: EEG, ERP, and neuroimaging studies. Psychological Bulletin, 132(2), 180–211. https://doi.org/10.1037/0033-2909.132.2.180

Haber, S. N., & Knutson, B. (2010). The reward circuit: Linking primate anatomy and human imaging. Neuropsychopharmacology, 35(1), 4–26. https://doi.org/10.1038/npp.2009.129

Mar, R. A., Oatley, K., & Hirsh, J. (2006). Bookworms versus nerds: Exposure to fiction versus non-fiction, divergent associations with social ability, and the simulation of fictional social worlds. Journal of Research in Personality, 40(5), 694–712. https://doi.org/10.1016/j.jrp.2005.08.002

Carter, C. S., & Porges, S. W. (2013). The biochemistry of love: An oxytocin hypothesis. EMBO Reports, 14(1), 12–16. https://doi.org/10.1038/embor.2012.191

Odendaal, J. S., & Meintjes, R. A. (2003). Neurophysiological correlates of affiliative behaviour between humans and dogs. The Veterinary Journal, 165(3), 296–301. https://doi.org/10.1016/S1090-0233(02)00237-X

Guastella, A. J., Mitchell, P. B., & Dadds, M. R. (2008). Oxytocin increases gaze to the eye region of human faces. Biological Psychiatry,

63(1), 3–5. https://doi.org/10.1016/j.biopsych.2007.06.026

Holt-Lunstad, J., Birmingham, W. A., & Light, K. C. (2008). Influence of a "warm touch" support enhancement intervention among married couples on ambulatory blood pressure, oxytocin, alpha amylase, and cortisol. Psychosomatic Medicine, 70(9), 976–985. https://doi.org/10.1097/PSY.0b013e318187aef7

Ditzen, B., Schaer, M., Gabriel, B., Bodenmann, G., Ehlert, U., & Heinrichs, M. (2009). Intranasal oxytocin increases positive communication and reduces cortisol levels during couple conflict. Biological Psychiatry, 65(9), 728–731. https://doi.org/10.1016/j.biopsych.2008.10.011

Feinberg, M., Willer, R., & Schultz, M. (2014). Gossip and ostracism promote cooperation in groups. Psychological Science, 25(3), 656–664. https://doi.org/10.1177/0956797613504626

Falk, E. B., Cascio, C. N., Coronel, J. C., & Leshin, R. A. (2014). Cognition and the senses: Olfaction as a model system for dual-process theories of cognitive psychology. Frontiers in Neurology, 5, 279. https://doi.org/10.3389/fneur.2014.00279

Riem, M. M., Bakermans-Kranenburg, M. J., Huffmeijer, R., van Ijzendoorn, M. H., & Parsons, C. E. (2013). Oxytocin effects on mind-reading are moderated by experiences of maternal love withdrawal: An fMRI study. Progress in Neuro-Psychopharmacology and Biological Psychiatry, 40, 273–280. https://doi.org/10.1016/j.pnpbp.2012.10.014

Csikszentmihalyi, M. (1990). Flow: The psychology of optimal experience. Harper & Row.

Moyer, C. A., Rounds, J., & Hannum, J. W. (2004). A meta-analysis of massage therapy research. Psychological Bulletin, 130(1), 3–18. https://doi.org/10.1037/0033-2909.130.1.3

Berk, L. S., Tan, S. A., Fry, W. F., Napier, B. J., Lee, J. W., Hubbard, R. W., Lewis, J. E., & Eby, W. C. (1989). Neuroendocrine and stress hormone changes during mirthful laughter. American Journal of the Medical Sciences, 298(6), 390–396.

Blood, A. J., & Zatorre, R. J. (2001). Intensely pleasurable responses to music correlate with activity in brain regions implicated in reward and emotion. Proceedings of the National Academy of Sciences, 98(20), 11818–11823. https://doi.org/10.1073/pnas.191355898

Macht, M., & Mueller, J. (2007). Immediate effects of chocolate on experimentally induced mood states. Appetite, 49(3), 667–674. https://doi.org/10.1016/j.appet.2007.05.004

Holick, M. F. (1995). Environmental factors that influence the cutaneous production of vitamin D. American Journal of Clinical Nutrition, 61(3), 638S–645S. https://doi.org/10.1093/ajcn/61.3.638S

Csikszentmihalyi, M. (1990). Flow: The psychology of optimal experience. Harper & Row.

Kim, D. (2018). The Effects of Sound Bath on Stress Reduction: A Pilot Study. Holistic Nursing Practice, 32(1), 29–36. https://doi.org/10.1097/hnp.0000000000000261

Seligman, M. E. P. (2002). Authentic Happiness: Using the New Positive Psychology to Realize Your Potential for Lasting Fulfillment. Simon & Schuster.

Furukawa, T. A., & Rosenbaum, J. F. (2018). The use of antidepressants for functional gastrointestinal disorders: a case-based review. Annals of Gastroenterology, 31(3), 260–269. https://doi.org/10.20524/aog.2018.0264

Harvard Health Publishing. (2020, August 13). Tryptophan. Harvard Health. https://www.health.harvard.edu/newsletter_article/Tryptophan

Nehlig, A., Daval, J. L., & Debry, G. (1992). Caffeine and the central nervous system: mechanisms of action, biochemical, metabolic and psychostimulant effects. Brain Research Reviews, 17(2), 139–170. https://doi.org/10.1016/0165-0173(92)90012-b

Raison, C. L., & Miller, A. H. (2011). Is depression an inflammatory disorder? Current Psychiatry Reports, 13(6), 467–475. https://doi.org/10.1007/s11920-011-0232-0

Meet the Author

Kathleen Evans is presently a Licensed Mental Health Counselor working at Cornell University in Ithaca, NY. She earned her B.A. in Psychology from the Catholic University of America and her M.S. in Counseling Psychology from SUNY Albany. Over the years, Evans has worked in a variety of job roles in the mental health field, including vocational counseling, in-home family counseling, outpatient behavioral health, private practice, and college counseling centers.

Evans utilizes psychoeducation, neuroscience, empowerment, and evidence-based practices to aid clients on their journey towards the greatest version of themselves. With humor and empathy, she uses a solution-focused, strength-based approach to holistic healing, starting with mindful awareness as a foundation. She believes in the power of healing for any individual through the practice of thought management, distress tolerance, and communication building. In her free time, you can find her enjoying the St. Lawrence River or watching the newest Bravo reality show.

Many thanks to you, the readers of,
Stop Overthinking and Boost Your Mood
Please ask for it
at your local library
or bookstore.

Reviews on
Amazon or Goodreads
are greatly appreciated.

Follow me on
LinkedIn

INSTAGRAM
@boostyourmoodbook

Contact me to schedule library or book club events.

www.ingramcontent.com/pod-product-compliance
Lightning Source LLC
LaVergne TN
LVHW012011060526
838201LV00061B/4269